# Run

## with
# Abandon

# Run
## with
# Abandon

## Restoring Your Childlike Joy
## and Trust in God

JILL McGAFFIGAN

*Run with Abandon: Restoring Your Childlike Joy and Trust in God*

by Jill McGaffigan

Published by HigherLife Development Services, Inc.
400 Fontana Circle
Building 1—Suite 105
Oviedo, Florida 32765
(407) 563-4806

Scriptures are taken from the HOLY BIBLE, NEW INTERNATIONAL VERSION®. NIV®. Copyright © 1973, 1978, 1984 by Biblica. Used by permission of Zondervan. All rights reserved.

ISBN 13: 978-1-935245-47-6
ISBN 10: 1-935245-47-3

First edition

12 13 14 15 — 9 8 7 6 5 4 3 2 1

Printed in the United States of America

As a parent of nineteen children, I have witnessed the simplicity of the joy, trust, and innocence they possess. When Jesus speaks, we would be wise to listen! Jill has listened and, with stories from her heart that bare her soul, Jill walks the reader through the process of learning how to run with abandon into the waiting arms of our heavenly Father. Life is complex, but Jesus calls us to live simply as His children. I encourage you to read this book and let the journey begin!

— *Pat Williams, Senior Vice President, Orlando Magic*

I have been privileged to know Jill McGaffigan for more than twenty years. Her sincere, caring, authentic, and loyal walk with the Savior has always been so inviting. When I see Jill, I see the Father! *Run with Abandon* is the overflow of Jill's quest to know and follow Jesus. She encourages you to fall into the arms of a God who cares. She challenges you to surrender to the One who loves you most and knows you best. *Run with Abandon* exposes her heart and reveals heaven's heart. Thanks, Jill, for sharing the deep waters that flow from your soul!

— *Tim Cash, Lead Pastor, The Oasis Church*
*www.theoasischurch.org, www.thetaramansion.net*

Jill McGaffigan is an artful storyteller. In *Run with Abandon*, she weaves stories of her personal experiences with biblical insights as she urges her readers to return to the pursuit of the right kind of relationship with the Father. It is a heartening and inspiring read.

— *Holly J. Carey, PhD, Associate Professor of Biblical Studies, Point University*

*Run with Abandon* stirred up one of my favorite stories from the Gospels, the Prodigal Son. I have read it many times, each time seeing God (the prodigal's Father) standing on the roof of the house, on the chimney, on tiptoes, watching for the return of his son. I can see the son and the Father running with the abandon that Jill describes so well. Jill's touching and real-life stories stirred that deep chord in my own soul that encourages me to run with a "carefree, almost reckless desire to know Him completely!" Jill's insights are powerful in the honest sharing of her own family life. I am gratefully reminded by Jill that God desires to be close to us in the easy and the tough times. *Run with Abandon* is a gift to all of us when we have drifted too far from the Father's love and discover it is time to go home.

— *W. David McEntire, Senior Pastor, First United Methodist Church*
*Lakeland, Florida*

Reading *Run with Abandon* will inspire you to consider the childlike qualities that made life simple in our relationships with others and, most importantly, with God. Jill paints a wonderful picture of the love Jesus has for each of His children through her experiences as a wife, a mom, "Grammy," a daughter, and a friend. As you read this book, I imagine you will envision Jesus with His arms open wide, waiting for you to run toward Him to enjoy the relationship God created us to enjoy."

— *Vince Nauss, President, Baseball Chapel*

How can one get so much out of such a simple thought as running to the Father with abandon? Perhaps it is because Jill's life experience has taught her that running to the Father is both simple and complex. As the facets on a diamond make it sparkle, the many facets exposed in this book make it sparkle. Reading this book is a stress reliever. It simplifies our cluttered lives. It says, "Relax, and go for it; He is waiting."

— *Bill Redmon, President, Removing the Barriers Initiative; former Executive Director, Lake Aurora Christian Camp and Retreat Center*

I have had the pleasure of knowing Jill and her husband, Andy, for many years. God has put this book on Jill's heart, and it is a message for today. In a world where we are told to grow up, Jill reminds us that Jesus wants us to have a childlike faith. In a world that says do, we learn how to be what God wants us to be.

— *Tom Roy, Founder/President, UPI (Unlimited Potential), a not-for-profit, 501(c)3 faith ministry*

# TABLE OF CONTENTS

# FOREWORD

C. S. Lewis said of George MacDonald, "I know hardly any writer who seems to be closer, or more continually close, to the Spirit of Christ Himself." In Jill McGaffigan, I find a kindred spirit. The Lord places a high value on childlike faith, and Jill's faith embodies that value. She lives a consistent, congruent, childlike life of faith. If you spend just five minutes with Jill, her laughter and joy will touch you. Out of her open heart and open life flows the very heart of Christ. Now she invites her reader to discover, or rediscover, the joy of knowing the Father. When she sheds tears, they reveal the longing of a daughter, a sister, and a friend for more of the shared goodness of the Father. More often than not, both her tears and her delight will be for you, her friend. Jill's vision and passion are to see Christ formed in her loved ones. In fact, she labors toward that end. *Run with Abandon* is a fruit of her labor of love.

Privileged to journey with Jill and her husband, Andy, I recall clearly her announcement that a book was being birthed within her. Jill's creative book has been fraught with trials, suffering, and confusion but comes from a heart that seeks more to know Christ through these difficulties than to understand why they are there. Like our Lord, she has learned a trusting obedience through her suffering.

A good book unlocks, opens, reveals, reaches, and stirs. Jill's book does all that—and more. In the opening pages, the reader senses her impassioned invitation to "grab the Father's hand," and the book progresses to the tearful good-bye to her precious mother at the book's close. From start to finish, I sensed the Father's wrapping His arms around me even before I could reach for His outstretched hand. The book immediately moved me to begin to change, as the Lord said plainly to His disciples in their quest for greatness: "Change and become like little children" (Matthew 18:3). This book helped me to identify the "weeds" from the "plant" inside me. I could see ways I play the martyr instead of relating directly. And the book helped me to move with the Spirit toward the release of the real me and uprooting of self-protective ways.

I felt like Ebenezer Scrooge as I engaged with Jill's words. My family's favorite rendition of this Dickens tale is *The Muppet Christmas Carol*. In this version, Scrooge is visited by two ghosts in chains, his former business partners, Jacob and Robert Marley, played by the curmudgeonly hecklers. They warn miserly Ebenezer with a haunting song that leaves a chilling directive echoing throughout the chambers of his bedroom and heart to change. Through the revelatory ministry of the three spirits, Scrooge is open to changing. When he awakes to find he has not missed Christmas morning,

Scrooge frolicks around his room in merriment. Jill's words reopened that same childlike joy and freedom in this curmudgeon's heart.

During our season of intense personal trials, the Spirit highlights our throbbing need. When we are hurting, our lives are rocked, and our faith is shaken. We need somewhere to go, someone to go to, Someone to know, and something to do.

Recently, I had just had a long after-hours emergency with one of my clients, which extended into the late night and the weekend. The next morning, I found myself exhausted and having a particularly difficult time focusing on the day before me and the people for whom I cared. As I began to move into a day that would have felt overwhelming even without the late-night work, dread and panic seized me. At that moment, I looked down and saw *Run with Abandon* on my desk and was reminded of the many perspectives Jill shares. I literally cracked a smile as I pictured myself reaching out to the needed "someone" who would help me connect to our "Someone" and sense His "something to do." In that moment, I joined in the joy of the struggle and the "run."

Jill's writing shows the reader this path to "run with abandon" through struggles, pain, and suffering into the arms of Christ Himself. In the process of our running, Jill reveals how the Father's arms are already preparing a way for us not only to cope or feel at peace, but also to have "something to do" to reach out to others even when our growth is a work in progress.

I not only love *Run with Abandon*, but it helped me. So whether you're a curmudgeon, a disciple, or both, grab the Father's hand, and join the journey back to your true childlike, Christlike nature. Curl up with Jill's book, and open your heart to the Spirit's "flashlight." Along the way, choose a safe "somebody" to walk alongside you. This is a path that leads us home—to our true home within our Father's heart, to our true life within His kingdom.

— Dr. Tom Petit,
Certified Clinical Mental Health Counselor,
Center for Biblical Counseling

www.drtompetit.com

# INTRODUCTION

I n the summer of 2004, I was awakened at 3 A.M. with the idea of this book in my head. Since I had never considered writing a book, this was an astounding phenomenon for me. I got out of bed and went to sit in the living room to consider the possibilities. Quickly, I realized it was the Lord who had placed this message in my mind and upon my heart. So immediately, I wrote the outline down in a journal and continued to marvel at what was happening. In the wee hours of the morning, I somehow understood this was not a project for immediate action, but rather a work God was doing inside of me. In the morning, I told my husband about the experience and then continued to ponder my next steps.

As I spent quiet time in reflection and prayer, I came to recognize that God had actually been "writing this book in me" for my entire life and that I had been living out and teaching the concepts throughout my lifetime. When I read over Bible study lessons I had prepared and taught for women's retreats, it became apparent that the book had been in the process for some time. As I shared the outline of the book with our children in the years to follow, they lightheartedly let me know the concepts were not foreign to them since they were enfolded in these concepts growing up in our home. All of this confirmed what I believed God was speaking to me. Also, it was incredibly humbling to recognize that this book had been in the process for years as the Master molded and shaped me for His purposes.

The message itself is not a new one, as it is clearly taught directly and conceptually throughout the Word of God. But God has intertwined my life experiences with the reality of the childlike relationship He desires to have with all of His creation in order to teach this important lesson in a new, fresh, and appealing manner.

In the years to follow, at each opportunity I had, I continued to teach what God laid on my heart, and I recognized the consistency in the theme of those messages. Also, I spent time reflecting on my relationship with my heavenly Father, meditating on His Word, and praying for direction and an understanding of the timing. During this time, it became apparent to me that God was preparing me to write this book in some ways that I did not find appealing. As I experienced serious health issues, personal family tragedies, and the loss of financial security due to circumstances beyond our control, I was brought to a new level of surrender to the Father. This surrender was not forced upon me, but I chose to relinquish my hold on my health, relationships, and finances as my source of security and chose the Lord God Almighty as my rock, my refuge, and my source of strength during those times of intense uncertainty. In hindsight, I can see how these experiences helped prepare me to write this book—which, I became acutely aware, I would do in God's time and not a minute sooner.

Two years ago, Andy and I felt we needed to pray for God to enable me to have time to go away to focus on writing. We tentatively planned several dates for this, only to realize it was impossible for me to leave our home or business at those times. Finally, a date approached that appeared to work for us, and Andy and I were more than ready to take a huge leap of faith. I wrote to a few close friends and asked them to pray for our needs to be met as the book came to fruition. Our good friend and Christian counselor Dr. Tom Petit had walked with us through our challenges for the previous seventeen years and with me through the seven-year book preparation time. He told me he believed I was about to "give birth," as he could see I was "full-term" and maybe even "in transition." He felt certain that the "birth" was approaching quickly. I knew what those terms meant because I was "full-term," and then some, with each of my babies. I was ready for the birthing process and felt Dr. Petit's words were a form of confirmation that the time was fast-approaching!

When the time came to write, I went to the mountain house that our parents left to my brothers and me. I had set aside two weeks to write, thinking I could get a good start on the book. It turns out, I wrote the entire book in five days! I was shocked and amazed that it simply spilled out of me and onto paper. I spent the second week doing some editing and then came home to begin finding a publisher. This was a daunting task, as I felt clueless as to how to proceed with this. I had some conversations with knowledgeable people, submitted a few proposals, interviewed with some prospects, and felt a nudge to commit to a specific publisher within a few months. Although the whirlwind seemed to be slowing down, there was still one major obstacle to overcome.

To move forward with the publisher, we needed to commit to buy a minimum number of books, which would be a challenge because financial resources were simply unavailable. However, Andy and I prayerfully relinquished any hold we may have had on this project to the capable hands of the Father. We had always discussed the fact that this book was not designed to bring glory to ourselves but to the Lord, and we recognized that once again it was time to trust in Him, rather than in our own efforts.

The meeting with the publisher was set for 4 P.M. one Thursday, and at 9 P.M. the night before, we had only a $1,000 investment from my aunt of the $5,500 required to move forward. That evening, a member of our church called my husband and asked him to come over to his house for a few minutes. When Andy came back, he was holding $4,000 from this friend, who believed the Lord had led him to invest in this project for the kingdom of God. Later, I opened the mail and realized another person had mailed us a check for the same purpose. The next day, a friend handed me cash, saying she and her husband believed God had led them to contribute. So when we left for our appointment, we had $5,350 in hand to give to the publisher, and he graciously accepted what we had and amended the contract to reflect the amount God had provided!

Besides the obvious, another interesting aspect of this story is it shows how well my heavenly Father knows me! If I had been able to write the check for the publishing contract out of our resources, I would have had moments of doubt as to whether this was the right time or the right publisher. As it is, I have no doubt God has ordained that this book be printed now. While I don't know the reasons, I am confident this is the perfect time for *Run with Abandon* to be made available to readers everywhere. It is my earnest prayer that this book remains a tool for promoting absolute adoration for and supreme submission to a loving heavenly Father, who is always waiting for His child to run to Him to experience the ultimate love relationship!

In His abundant love,

Jill

# CHAPTER 1

# RUN LIKE CRAZY

I have a very clear picture in my head of my grandson Tristan's coming to see me, "Grammy," after a long time apart. It was at my favorite place this side of heaven, the North Carolina mountain house my parents left my two brothers and me when they passed away. From the house, a long drive leads to a beautiful meadow. On one side of the meadow, a path winds to a pond, while a creek meanders along the opposite side of the meadow.

When the kids arrived, Tristan asked to get out of the car as soon as he saw me in the meadow, waving at him. They stopped the car, and he jumped out. He was so excited, he forgot to close the door behind him. He took off down the embankment and ran across the field to where I stood by the pond. His arms were wide open, and his face revealed his pure delight. He ran with all the energy he could muster. Tristan paid no attention to holes or rocks that he could have tripped over because at that moment, he cared about only one thing: reaching the object of his affection!

I was kneeling with my arms open wide to receive him, fully expecting to be knocked over upon impact. When Tristan rested within my embrace, he said, "I love you, Grammy" . . . and he knew I loved him too.

This is a reflection of the way we are to enthusiastically seek our heavenly Father. Like I was for Tristan, He is always waiting, desiring for us to run to Him with this kind of abandon . . . a carefree, almost reckless desire to know Him completely!

When answering a question His disciples asked, Jesus explained the need for His followers to interact in a childlike relationship with the Father. The Bible tells it like this in Matthew 18:1–4:

> *The disciples came to Jesus and asked, "Who is the greatest in the kingdom of heaven?" He called a little child and had him stand among them. And he said: "I tell you the truth, unless you change and become like little children, you will never enter the kingdom of heaven. Therefore, whoever humbles himself like this child is the greatest in the kingdom of heaven."*

I can imagine that Jesus' response may have shocked these manly men! To become humble and "like little children" probably was not what they were expecting to hear, and those traits may not have appeared to be God-honoring at first glance. Furthermore, Jesus pointed out that this would mean their changing. Many of us do not like the idea of change unless it is our idea. Thus, the need for humility becomes apparent. The disciples also may have had trouble grasping the concept of becoming childlike if they equated that with childishness. While most people would expect people to outgrow many irresponsible behaviors with maturity, Jesus wanted His followers to grasp the connection between childlikeness and a pure love relationship with our heavenly Father. In fact, Jesus told His disciples that "whoever humbles himself like this child is the greatest in the kingdom of heaven."

However, when we ponder the relationship we have with the only perfect parent, our heavenly Father, we realize how much we have strayed from being like little children—who are innocent, trusting, eager to learn, pure in motive, and unencumbered, who express emotion easily, who have needs, and who have yet to become entangled with sin. He understands the struggle we face in letting go of the things we have allowed to bind us. He also knows how difficult it is for us to find freedom by allowing these childlike traits to reach the surface of our lives. Finally, the Father understands it is challenging for us to love Him with the same kind of submissive obedience a child who recognizes the authority of his parent has. Yet, He desires it.

Personally, when I have submitted in this way, I have found the comfort I have needed at the exact times I have needed it the most. My husband played professional baseball for fourteen years, beginning in 1978, which included the privilege of playing at the major-league level from 1981 to 1991. So when I married Andy, I knew moving was a natural part of a baseball player's life. As we began having children, obviously the load increased when it came time to take a trip. Traveling by car is difficult enough with the extra paraphernalia children need, but at least we have a choice as to who sits where. Furthermore, if the noise level gets out of hand, we find comfort in knowing it only annoys the family, not strangers sitting in close proximity. This is not the case on an airplane.

However, I had flying alone with my children down to a science. One child was neatly tucked into the car seat with a teddy bear and a pacifier, while the other occupied my lap and my full attention. The diaper bag was like a bag of tricks. I had the perfect toys, food, and drinks for any occasion. Despite all my preparations, some of my trips did not go according to plan.

On one such occasion, I was traveling to my parents' home for a couple of weeks while my husband was on a road trip. The first leg of the journey, the longest, was fairly uneventful, except the flight arrived late and made my connecting time very tight. Confidently, I gathered my belongings with every intention of making the next flight. I carried a car seat in my right hand and had my three-year-old daughter hold that pinkie. I carried the diaper bag over my left shoulder and my heavy year-old son in my left arm. Next, I ran to an entirely different concourse and arrived before the doors closed.

I was out of breath and energy but relieved that we made the flight. Though no one offered to assist me, I bumped my way down the aisle to my seat in the last row of the plane. Then I settled the kids in and took a deep breath while whispering a prayer of thanksgiving.

While the second leg of the trip was only thirty minutes, it ended up feeling more like thirty hours. As soon as we took off, my youngest began to cry. Nothing would pacify him; he would only cry harder. (In fact, I didn't know a child could cry that hard for that long.) I received nothing but dirty looks from those around me as they seemed to be thinking, *Can't you control your spoiled children?* When I got off the plane, all I could do was hand my children to my mom and fall into my daddy's arms for a good cry. At that moment, I knew I was safe and secure and everything would be fine.

Many times in my life, I have thought I've had it all together, only to find my well-made plans crumble in an instant. During such times of crisis or disappointment, while I am no longer able to fall into my earthly daddy's arms, I *can* fall into the arms of my heavenly Father. At any moment, I am able to experience the love of God if I choose to turn to Him, and I can be confident that I will receive His comfort. I can be certain that I am eternally safe and secure, and no matter what happens in this life, everything ultimately will be fine. The question is, Will I choose to turn to Him?

With words like "love" and "cry," it may be uncomfortable for some of you to read further. But before you close this book, take a moment to consider the origin of the topic. This book is based on a bold command Jesus gave to His followers—the twelve men He had chosen as disciples—during His earthly ministry, in response to a question they asked. This group was comprised of a variety of personality types and education levels—fishermen, a tax collector, and a doctor, to name a few. Their question, "Who is the greatest?" is typical of strong-willed, goal-oriented people who want to know what must be accomplished to get a job done and how to be the best while doing it. Perhaps it is helpful to keep in mind that Jesus Himself was not wimpy or sappy, but a strong, authoritative, courageous Man who was confident about who He was as well as the purpose for His life. Jesus sweat during His manual labor as a carpenter, turned over tables in the temple when righteous anger consumed Him, stood His ground against the accusations of the temple authorities, and withstood forty lashes before dying on a cross when He had the opportunity to save Himself from a gruesome death. This is not the picture of a coward—but of a very capable Man!

However, this is the same Man who wept in public for His dead friend, held children on His knee, and showed compassion and tenderness to hurting people. Within the Person of Jesus, we see the perfect picture of a stalwart Man who was still His Father's child within. Jesus taught His followers the true meaning of love by living His life remaining in a healthy relationship with the Father. Jesus challenged His disciples daily to accept

God's definition of love and His methodology for achieving love in its purest form by following His example.

Today, it is up to us to move forward in a quest to follow Jesus' example of childlikeness by unearthing the traits that have been buried throughout our lifetime. It would be wise to explore the meaning of Jesus' words when He said we must "change and become like little children." What exactly must we change, and how did we get away from childlikeness in the first place? If we decide to venture in that direction, we will need to explore how to do it and what the end result will look like. These are some of the topics we will delve into in the chapters that follow. So slip on your shoes, and come along on the journey. The Father is waiting for each of His children to choose to open the door of the heart and run like crazy, with wild abandon, toward His welcoming embrace.

# STUDY GUIDE

1. Does the phrase "run to Him with this kind of abandon . . . a carefree, almost reckless desire to know Him completely" describe your relationship with God? Explain your response.

2. What emotions well up inside of you when you consider running with abandon to the Father?

3. In response to the question the disciples asked Jesus about greatness, what do you think He was trying to convey to them? If you were in their shoes, how do you imagine you would have felt about the answer Jesus gave?

4. How do your heart and mind respond to the idea of your running into the arms of God as a father figure? How would you describe your image of God as your Father?

# CHAPTER 2

# RUNNING THE BASES

As Andy progressed through the minor leagues early in his career, he was blessed to be in the New York Yankee organization. Because this organization makes excellence a high priority, it meant some incredibly talented men coached and mentored Andy. When I met my husband, I did not know much about baseball, so attending spring training practices and games was a great opportunity to learn. I noticed something interesting that didn't change as Andy progressed from rookie ball to the big leagues: Each spring, at every level, the teams participated in drills to practice the basics of the game.

The daily spring training practices consisted of such things as running the bases, fielding ground balls, hitting, and pitching. I could understand the need for these simple exercises in little league, but I had assumed that these were well-learned skills by the time an athlete reached the professional level. However, I came to understand that if a player is able to master these basic skills, he is more likely to successfully handle the many challenging plays he encounters throughout the long baseball season. Therefore, the players practiced. Certainly, this intricate and sometimes mundane training can be tied to Andy's later successes in baseball.

Like with baseball, we must practice the basic principles of this life if we expect to reflect them in our daily living. Throughout His earthly ministry, Jesus laid out these basics for us. In addition to the disciples' asking, "Who is the greatest in the kingdom of heaven?" a lawyer asked Jesus, "Teacher, which is the greatest commandment in the Law?" (Matthew 22:36). Jesus responded: "'Love the Lord your God with all your heart and with all your soul and with all your mind.' This is the first and greatest commandment. And the second is like it: 'Love your neighbor as yourself.' All the Law and the Prophets hang on these two commandments" (vv. 37–40). This command is important to the subject of this book because it prioritizes our love relationships. We must love God above everything and everyone, without exception. Then, we must love ourselves in a healthy way so we are capable of loving others. As we explore changing to become like children, we will discover that this God-defined love we are pursuing will encompass many of the qualities involved in childlikeness. Because we reach physical maturity, it does not necessarily mean we have a flawless understanding of love relationships. Just as a professional athlete continues his training throughout his career, it is crucial we recognize the need for ongoing education and practice in the art of love throughout our lifetime. With love, we never get to a point where we have arrived at our destination while we still draw breaths in this world. The battle for our loyalties in love is very real, and I believe this is why Jesus pointed out the need to love God with all of our being!

Considering this, what better time is there for mankind to seek our heavenly Father with all of our heart, soul, and mind? After all, we are surrounded by cruelty, depravity, and brashness. We can hardly get away from seeing or hearing related local and world events on the radio, on TV, on the Internet, and through other live venues of communication made readily available everywhere. We constantly hear about people who are "lovers of themselves, lovers of money, boastful, proud, abusive, disobedient to their parents, ungrateful, unholy, without love, unforgiving, slanderous, without self-control, brutal, not lovers of the good, treacherous, rash, conceited, lovers of pleasure rather than lovers of God." Sound familiar? Those words are found in the New Testament, in 2 Timothy 3:2–4. They were written more than two thousand years ago, referring to the "terrible times in the last days" (v. 1). But, oh, how fitting they are in the world today!

We see and hear about the reality of this passage on a regular basis. Headlines tell of the parents who killed their children . . . and children who killed their parents. We hear about teenagers who have plotted, sometimes successfully, to kill their classmates over the loss of a boyfriend or girlfriend. Lying, cheating, and stealing are not the least bit uncommon, and when we hear about these things, we are almost relieved that nothing worse happened. We learn of depraved adults who, for their sexual pleasure, prey upon young children. Besides what we hear in the news, countless children cry themselves to sleep every night as they listen to the adults in the house fighting. Other little ones are treated with disrespect on a daily basis. Still other children's parents or guardians run illegal home-based businesses. And sadly, many children have never enjoyed the simple pleasure of getting a tender hug or of having a book read to them before bedtime. Today, too many children are growing up in an unhealthy home void of loving parental figures. For these children, and mankind as a whole, the only answer is to seek a thriving, passionate, insatiable relationship with almighty God!

We must recognize this is urgent and realize it is time to start the adventure of becoming as little children in order to love God and others in a way that is healthy and pleasing to the Father. God never intended for our relationship with Him to be complicated. Instead, He has always desired a sincere, simple, childlike rapport. Whether we admit it or not, it is imperative that we authentically know the only true God personally to survive life on this earth and ensure life with Him for eternity. Every one of us must choose whether we will accept the Father for who He is and, if we accept Him, how we will relate to Him. There is no question, God our Father desires this, as He has pursued a love relationship with His creation from the beginning of time. But in His wisdom, He has given us free will to reject His great and marvelous love or to accept it and journey through life in relationship with Him. After all, love is not love at all if it has been coerced. My mom used to tell me love must be given and received freely. She explained that it is best to let go of, not to clutch tightly, the object of my love. Then, if that person freely returns to the relationship, it will be genuine; if not, it was never really love. So it is with God. He lets His precious children have the freedom to choose or reject His pure love.

The outcome of our choosing to pursue the Father is outlined in Galatians 5:22–23: "The fruit of the Spirit is love, joy, peace, patience, kindness, goodness, faithfulness, gentleness and self-control." This is not to say that every person who calls himself a Christian will exhibit these traits, as ongoing practice is required for them to be developed. However, it is to say that the more we obediently follow the way of life Jesus taught, the more we will demonstrate these characteristics. It seems we often hear others describe the love, joy, and peace a person experiences during a time of crisis, as if that is the only time a Christian should show those characteristics. However, evidence of these traits should not be a strange phenomenon or reserved only for the difficult moments in life. It is an error to have such a low expectation concerning the outcome of our pursuit of the Father. This "fruit" can be on exhibit and enjoyed every day, as it will be a direct result of our daily regimen of "practice." Those who interact with us will benefit from this sweet fruit as we become vessels God can use to nourish the hungry souls in our world. We are equipped to love God and others as we pursue the Father in earnest. The truth is we can obtain all of these traits in abundance, and much more, as we walk hand in hand with Him in our quest toward childlikeness! Furthermore, eternity will find us continuing this unending love relationship in its purest form as we, in our childlikeness, finally meet the Father face to face in a glorious union!

On the other hand, a person who chooses not to pursue the Father is left prey to the hopelessness found in the world. Even a believer in God or someone who verbally aligns himself or herself with the teachings of Jesus may, unfortunately, choose to live life according to the demands of fleshly desires. For a Christian, maintaining a healthy, committed walk is very hard work, and following the easier path of our natural desires is certainly a temptation. As unintentional as taking the easy path may be, the effect inevitably will be that the person's life becomes a reflection of the world's, rather than God's, character. Some people choose to flat-out reject a relationship with the one true God. In both cases, the person is like a piece of fruit growing in the wild. Sometimes seeds fall in a favorable growing environment and are able to take root and produce a harvest. Once I remember finding watermelons growing in a pasture near my home. How the seeds were sown is a mystery, but it was obvious they were not planted intentionally or in any order. Nevertheless, the afternoon rain and fertile soil provided the basic requirements for the watermelons to grow. In the same way, people who choose to live apart from God are certainly capable of producing good things in this life, at least for a season. Unfortunately, it seems more common that very ugly traits become increasingly apparent as the person ages and the challenges of life increase. For some, the ability to make a satisfactory income is gone due to health or economic issues. Others may face a long, drawn-out illness that depletes resources and energy. For everyone, the process of aging diminishes the youthful appearance that some people have based their self-worth upon or have depended upon for their livelihood. The degree to which such a person chooses to indulge in the mind-set, pleasures, and passions of the flesh, and of the world, is the degree to which that person will exhibit traits common to the world. Unfortunately, the way of the world offers no hope for true love, joy, and inner peace, or for a life that is everlasting.

God has been teaching me these lessons since my birth, and in a way He has been writing this book in me throughout my entire life. I was blessed to have been born into a Christian home, and naturally, that environment influenced the person I am today. However, by virtue of living in this world, I was certainly affected by sin as I grew in stature. From the sins of those close to me, to my own personal struggles and sinful choices, to the evil of the world, life experiences have molded me, just like they have everyone else.

I believe God's intent for this book is to open my eyes, along with those of its readers, to the fact that we have all become something other than what God created us to be. The Father desires a healthy relationship with each of His children and is always waiting for us to reach out our hand to His. But at some level, the load we carry hinders us in our efforts to reach for Him. Everyone has journeyed from a different place and perhaps is carrying all of life's burdens on his or her shoulders. This is quite a heavy load for many of us. Therefore, maybe the journey has left us tired, weak, and thirsty. As you read the following chapters, it is my prayer that the words will bring rest and nourishment to your soul while making you hungrier than ever to know God more completely than you do now. When we choose to put down our cumbersome baggage and reach for the waiting hand of the Father, the next step will be the journey of reshaping. And in so doing, we will find He will receive us with warmth.

# STUDY GUIDE

1. Read Matthew 22:34–40.


2. What people or things "battle" for your personal loyalties in the area of love?


3. Which aspects of the fruit of the Spirit do you regularly exhibit in your life, and which ones do you need to exhibit more?


4. Think about the times when, intentionally or unintentionally, you have taken the easier path of yielding to the desires of the flesh and the ways of the world. How would you describe your relationship with your heavenly Father during those times?


5. What regularly hinders your sense of urgency to make, or keep, a love relationship with the Father your top priority?


6. Think about the symptoms of extreme physical hunger or thirst. Which of those descriptive words apply to your longing for a deeper love relationship with God?


7. Read Psalm 63.

# CHAPTER 3

# RUNNING THE COURSE

Unless we are paying close attention, the transformation from our original, childlike state can be subtle, and we may not even notice it. As an example, soon after our wedding, I witnessed such a change in my husband. Andy and I married in January, had a honeymoon, and came home to prepare for spring training. Needless to say, that was an exciting time in my life! After a two-year engagement and seemingly endless separation, I was able to live with the man of my dreams. Furthermore, we were off on an exciting adventure that we hoped would lead to a fulfilling career in baseball. No matter the trials before us, the fact that we were in this together was a consolation to me.

With a minor-league contract, we didn't have much money, so we were careful with our spending. Having only one car was a challenge, but we managed. I attended every home game to be close to Andy, and I was getting an inside look at the game of baseball. Unfortunately, that education extended beyond the field and the front office. At some point midway through the season, I began to wonder what happened to that fun-loving, joke-cracking, easygoing guy I had dated. Somehow, in the craziness of our life together, he had practically disappeared. I kept my concerns to myself because I honestly could not identify my feelings well enough to verbalize them.

Relief came in the off-season. I literally woke up one day and realized my "boyfriend" was back. Therefore, it didn't take a whole lot of figuring to add things up. Baseball season created a mountain of stress in my husband's world to which I was oblivious while sitting on my cloud. Andy had temporarily allowed the concerns of his job to burden him in such a way that it radically altered his typical behavior. While the loss and recapture of this particular trait spanned a short period of time, it was a challenge to overcome throughout his career. The lesson for us all in this story is that every one of us is affected by the events that take place in our lives. Who we are today is a result of happenings from our birth to this very moment. There are areas at our core in which we have become something other than who God created and intended for us to be.

Given that fact, it is good to ponder what Jesus meant when He stated rather strongly that we must "change and become like little children" to enter the kingdom of heaven. Change does not seem to be an option if we desire a pure relationship with the Father. Remember, children had no status in society in the place and time in which Jesus lived and, depending on their gender and parentage, may have held little value to their family. These factors must have held some significance in Jesus' choosing children, rather than politicians or scholars, for us to become like. Therefore, as we relate to God, we must not believe our worthiness is based on our education or status in the community. Rather, the Father loves us because we are His children.

Little children have certain qualities simply because they are children. They are newly created with a life ahead that is a clean slate. Immediately, the writing on that slate begins. In fact, children learn without even being aware that class is in session. With them, everything about life is a lesson. Each new day, children learn a little more about the world in which they live. I believe this is where the loss of those childlike traits begins. But this concept gets tangled up with the reality that many traits of a child need to be left behind, as childish behavior in an adult is not appealing. We place a word like "maturity" into the mix, but we may forget that emotional and spiritual maturity depend on many factors aside from the passing of years.

For example, we may make the mistake of thinking that spiritual maturity grows with age. However, I have known young people with the spiritual maturity of someone twice their age. Also, I have been acquainted with older folks who seem to be lacking in this area. Clearly, age does not determine spiritual maturity.

In the book of John, Jesus says we are to be "born again," and someone in the crowd raised the obvious question concerning this rebirth. This educated man made the observation that we cannot reenter the womb and be born a second time. Jesus explained that we are to experience a spiritual rebirth through a relationship with Him. Similarly, we cannot physically become a child for a second time. However, we are able to redeem the childlike qualities that once came naturally. As difficult as this may sound, it must be possible, or Jesus would not have commanded that it be done. Just as we do not become followers of the Lord Jesus Christ without making a personal decision to do so, we cannot "become like little children" without learning what that looks like and making it our goal.

Once we decide to run to the Father, or at least stroll in that direction, the journey and the hard work must begin. The journey will last a lifetime because as long as we live in our earthly bodies, we will struggle with the flesh's influence in our lives. We seem to be tempted constantly to indulge in activities that give us pleasure or to succumb to the pressures of this life. This enticement of our human nature can be extremely powerful indeed. If we believe the Bible is our guide to a God-honoring lifestyle, then we need to tenaciously deal with these desires and temptations by using it under the tutelage of the Father through prayer and reflection. In so doing, we will learn that we do not have to be a slave to these yearnings, but they will entangle us as long as we attempt to overcome them on our own. This influence of the flesh is why the work will be hard. It takes great discipline to make the wise choice to discover what the Spirit of God longs for and to act accordingly, rather than give in to the things the flesh craves or our natural areas of weakness.

As we run this course, it is important to recognize that our study of the Bible will reveal many names that describe the Almighty. Throughout this book, I have used many of these interchangeably, so before we delve too much further into the subject of childlikeness, it may be helpful to explain some of the names of God. Also, note that the term "god," lowercased, can be used when speaking of things we have given high importance to other than almighty God. The name I have used most often in this book is "Father," as it fits with the topic of a father-child relationship. But our heavenly Father is also the almighty Creator, who spoke the universe into existence and who appeared both in flesh, in the Person of Jesus Christ, and spirit form, in the Holy Spirit. "Lord" often appears as a name for God and depicts His authority over all the earth. At times, we may choose other authorities as lord. However, it does not negate the fact that God Almighty is Lord over all things! Many other synonyms appear in the Bible, and each one reveals a character trait found in the one true God. This is also the same all-powerful, all-knowing, ever-present God who is available to us in dealing with this conflict between our flesh and the Spirit God placed within each of us.

In addition, there are references to the battle that exists between our flesh and our own spirit. This battle is really more like a raging war! The attempted influence of Satan, a spiritual entity who is God's enemy, complicates that reality all the more. Once we have decided to walk hand in hand with God, the Spirit of almighty God does battle on our behalf on both fronts. We can be confident of our victory, as *the* Authority, or the Almighty, outranks all other authority in the heavenly realms and on earth. This all sounds simple until we begin to identify what the battle within ourselves is really all about. Romans 8:5 describes the Christian's dilemma this way: "Those who live according to the sinful nature have their minds set on what that nature desires; but those who live in accordance with the Spirit have their minds set on what the Spirit desires." Based on this, we win or lose this battle depending on what we think about, as the battle begins in our minds. Naturally, everything we have experienced in our past and what we are currently encountering influence what we think about. While these events may become obstacles on this new path we are exploring, we always have the option of redirecting and reprogramming our minds to overcome the obstacles.

For example, throughout our lives, what we read, see on television, listen to on the radio, and watch at the movies form in part our ideas concerning relationships. The war between good and evil is a popular topic for humankind to explore, as evidenced by the fact that it can be seen as the basis of most movie plots. I enjoy a good "chick flick," especially if the setting is Europe in the sixteenth, seventeenth, or eighteenth century. The whole idea of kings and lords involved with the queens and ladies attending balls and riding horseback seems incredibly romantic—until I stop to consider the odor of a ballroom or the reality of chamber pots. As well, a romantic interlude on a ship or deserted island seems attractive until I am reminded of such discomforts and maladies as insects, bad weather, and dysentery! While we may acknowledge that certain things only happen in the movies, we must admit that the things we have allowed to enter our minds over our lifetime may have skewed our views about life.

Another obstacle we may face revolves around our view of love, which all our life experiences have also formed. Each relationship that has involved the words "I love you"—whether with a parent, a child, a husband, a wife, a boyfriend, a girlfriend, or a best friend—has influenced our thinking. We have inflicted and experienced emotional pain, and we have treasured memories of love expressed in a gratifying way. Whether or not those relationships lasted, we must evaluate the impact of the good and bad memories on our view of love, as they remain entrenched in our mind's eye and deep in our soul. Personally, music greatly influences my thought and emotional processes—including when it comes to love. How many different ways songwriters describe love has struck me time and again, and some of those ways have truly hit the proverbial "nail on the head"—so much so that I often have felt I could sing their songs in worship to the Lord! In contrast, other songs reflect bitterness, anguish, and even a hateful response to an ended love relationship. Those songs perfectly illustrate the battle we face between thinking and living according to our flesh and according to our spirit. The fact is, we have a deep desire to love and to be loved, and our Creator placed that desire within our being.

Also, we may have a difficult time receiving the love the Father offers to us because we may mistakenly believe our worthiness of that love is based on our goodness. So if we harbor shame related to past relationships deep inside, we may find it hard to believe we deserve God's love. This error in our thinking may have formed as a result of our flesh, or natural tendency to give our love to others based on their performance. This reflects a lack of understanding that it is possible to wholeheartedly love someone while disapproving of a behavior or lifestyle. For example, a parent will not stop loving a toddler because the child is disobedient. But because we seem to become less gracious in our forgiveness of others as we become adults, naturally, we expect God will become less forgiving toward us. Even though mankind will never be without sin and is certainly unworthy of God's love, He still offers His children unconditional love, without reservation, while hating the sinful behavior. If we are able to accept this definition of "love" that God has provided for us, we will have a better chance of overcoming this love obstacle. As we agree to do the hard work this journey involves, the Lord is ready and willing to teach us about His true character.

In addition to becoming aware of the obstacles we will face along the way, we must know the beginning and the end points of the journey. If we believe there is a need to redeem our childlike qualities, then first we must understand how we lost them in the first place. Imagine being blindfolded and dropped off in the middle of the country. If you have a specific destination in mind, it is impossible to set a correct course without finding out where you are and understanding where you have been. The starting point of this journey is to admit we have lived long enough in this world to recognize it has adversely affected us. Each of us was born into a family not of our choosing, and we have had experiences in our formative years that have affected our development one way or another. So the process of losing our childlikeness began at birth. Which traits have been lost, when they were lost, and to what degree depend upon many things, including a person's choices, the choices of those around that person, and the environment in which the person was raised.

One of my favorite places to tour is Colonial Williamsburg in Virginia. I have fond memories of several visits with my mother, aunt, husband, and children. The experience is like stepping back in time to the early years of our nation's history. Without modern transportation and technology, life takes on a much slower pace, which in itself makes the time spent there worthwhile. Another prominent memory is of the little fenced or walled gardens next to many of the homes patterned after the ones around the magnificent estates in England. While meandering through these gardens, I am always overcome with a sense of tranquility that is rare for me. Every time I have had the opportunity to take a relaxing stroll through any garden, I have been acutely aware of the time, energy, and tender care it takes to plant and keep such a place. In my wildest daydreams, I have visualized a series of paths and landscaping in our own Florida backyard that would resemble these gardens, all the while knowing the requirements were too great for our family to handle. Therefore, it remains a pleasant thought that I can enjoy in my dreams.

Tending these gardens is a lot like reclaiming our lost childlike traits. Before a new flowerbed is planted, the gardener must make preparations. This may include tilling, plowing, and fertilizing the ground in the chosen area to be sure rocks and weeds are removed and the soil is ready for the seeds. The gardener digs holes in carefully chosen areas to allow for optimum growth, places seeds in the soil, pats down the earth, and supplies the right amount of water. The seedlings are fragile when they first sprout, but the garden begins to take on a special kind of beauty.

As the bed becomes more secure, plants need less water and are not as vulnerable to the environment. However, they still need attention, such as regular weeding. This is a fairly simple process, as the weeds are easy to spot and the roots are shallow, making them easy to remove. However, if the weeds are neglected, weed-pulling becomes more difficult and tedious because the weeds grow deeper and begin to intermingle with the roots of the young plants. Sometimes the weeds even become entangled with the plant above ground, making it difficult to uproot without disturbing the flower itself. Certain types of weeds grow close to the ground and can even prevent the gardener from seeing them. Other weeds are pretty, like a flowering plant, which gives them a sort of camouflage, but are still damaging to the plant. In fact, the flower may die due to a lack of nourishment as the weeds consume nutrients meant for the flower or hinder transportation of the nutrients to the flower as its root system deteriorates. This process can happen quickly, which is why a garden must be well-tended. Many times a master gardener, educated through intense training programs and many volunteer service hours, is hired for that purpose.

We were all very much like these newly planted flowers when God created us with a similar type of attentiveness and tenderness that a master gardener exhibits as he plants and cares for a garden. The writer of Psalm 139 describes beautifully God's creation of our being: "For you created my inmost being; you knit me together in my mother's womb. I praise you because I am fearfully and wonderfully made; your works are wonderful, I know that full well. My frame was not hidden from you when I was made in the secret place. When I was woven together in the depths of the earth, your eyes saw my unformed body" (vv. 13–16). God made us unique, and loves us uniquely!

But weeds have taken root in our hearts and may or may not have been tended to, depending on our childhood environment. Even in the best of situations growing up, some of the weeds would have grown up within us because no homes or parents are perfect. What has developed from a lack of tending to the garden of our soul has affected and will affect our minds, hearts, actions, speech, and relationships. Neglecting our spiritual life or not caring about our spiritual growth can do great damage to others and us. Unfortunately, we may not notice the effects of this neglect until the undesirable weeds produce fruit and become obvious. We realize that this distasteful fruit adversely affects our relationships with those around us. Therefore, it is imperative that we look for the weeds that we have allowed to grow within our soul and decide if we really like what we see.

So the starting point of this journey is to acknowledge to ourselves and to the Lord that from the time of our birth, the misdeeds of others, our own choices, and the evil in the world have influenced us. We were all once children, and whether or not we were exposed to intentional abuse, every child has been exposed to people who did not treat, teach, or care for them properly. Likewise, following our own desires for personal satisfaction and pleasure did not always cultivate attractive qualities in us. No one is exempt from the outcome. Because of these experiences, we have made assumptions and drawn conclusions about who we are and even about our self-worth. Every experience has either confirmed or nullified those assumptions and conclusions. Those experiences have created unhealthy patterns of behavior that leave us ill-equipped, in varying degrees, for interaction with God and others. Our soul has been marred and tainted in deep places that no one around us can see. In fact, even *we* may be blind to the damage.

Despite this, the good news is we have access to the true master Gardener, almighty God, and all we have to do is ask, and He will help. Furthermore, we can begin this important work immediately, as our heavenly Father accepts us as we are today. Because He is intimately acquainted with every aspect of our being, He has complete understanding of the "weeds" that are tangled in the "good seeds" planted within each of us. Also, He knows how to pull those weeds precisely, and while it may turn up a bit of soil in the process, His methods will allow for the proper nourishment of those deeply rooted qualities He planted in the beginning. However, for this work to begin in us, we must ask for the master Gardener's help. Because we are not puppets, the Father will not barge into a person's life uninvited. Instead, we have free will and must choose whether to allow this tedious tending of the garden of our hearts. Our attitude makes all the difference, and God promises to empower His people when they choose a path of faith in Him. Therefore, we must run with our arms wide open toward the Father for liberation, healing, and transformation and begin the process of redeeming what has been lost. Even when we do, often we will not see the results of this quest instantly.

Shortly before writing this book, I burned my thumb badly. The pain was excruciating, and it didn't take long for blisters to form. Because blisters are the body's way of protecting the burned area from infection, I carefully kept it bound and consistently used antibiotic cream to help prevent infection. About ten days later, the skin that had formed the blisters began to dry, and it eventually peeled off. I was amazed at the softness and tenderness of that new skin. Unfortunately, some areas sustained permanent damage.

In our lives, when we grant God permission, He will show us the source of our pain, bring healing to our wounds, and transform us into children who are once again soft and tender toward Him. When our experiences have resulted in permanent consequences, He is still able to mold a willing heart while providing the comfort of His love and never-ending presence. No matter where we are today, we have the opportunity to begin this journey for the first time or start where we left off and explore the vast possibilities in becoming more childlike. We can do this by choosing to travel with the Father on this sometimes bumpy road that has been marred by our personal flesh battles, our skewed thinking, and the subtle, unintentional changes to our childlikeness.

# STUDY GUIDE

1. Begin to make a list of events in your life that may have contributed to smothering your childlike traits. Add to the list as you progress through the book.

2. Read and think about Romans 8:1–17.

3. What do you regularly think about that may serve as an obstacle to the process of reclaiming your childlike qualities?

4. What experiences have had a positive or negative effect on your view of love and your worthiness of love?

5. Read Psalm 139, and make a list of the personal ways your heavenly Father has been and would like to be involved in your life.

# CHAPTER 4

# RUNNING FOR THE GOAL

Our son Drew loves to be involved in various outdoor sports that make me a little nervous. One of his favorite activities is hiking on the Appalachian Trail, and he has been known to go on weeklong hikes alone. While I anxiously watch him make detailed preparations, he assures me he really isn't alone, that God is surely in the midst of nature, and other hikers are on the trail as well. If you're a mother, you probably understand why I still worry about my son's safety.

Once when I dropped Drew off at the head of the trail for a one-week trek alone, I asked him about the painted white mark on the side of a tree. He told me the trail was well-marked with the familiar blaze to keep hikers on the correct path, as animals and hikers have created many side trails over the years. This was incredibly reassuring, as I knew he desired to stay on the trail and reach his destination on time. Also, it was comforting to know where to start looking if he didn't show up at our rendezvous at the end of the week.

Like my son, we must grab the Father's hand and take off on the trail that He has so clearly outlined for us! I recommend prayerfully reading these next pages and asking the Father to reveal the areas where you should begin your trek. There is no quick way to our spiritual growth, just as a child cannot go from age six to sixteen overnight. (If it were possible to reach age sixteen more quickly, I'm sure I would have figured out how!) Just as physical and emotional growth spurts occur in our lives, we may experience fast-paced, exhilarating, and rewarding spiritual growth at the onset of our journey. However, we must be prepared for the slower growth periods as well. That's because certain traits take time and life experience to develop. We must be patient and allow the Lord's timing to be our timing! Of course, for most of us, this is easier said than done.

Nowadays, people are used to getting what they want immediately. In fact, much of life seemingly is centered on the knowledge that all of our needs can be met by pushing a few buttons on a mobile device keypad, though for many of us older folks, it is hard to grasp this concept. While I was working on this book, our daughter, Robin, was studying to be a teacher and had written some excellent lesson plans the previous couple of years. I asked her if she was keeping those lesson plans in a file box so she could use them when she has a teaching position someday. She heartily laughed and said, "No, Momma. I have them saved on a flash drive." We both had a good belly laugh as I once again realized my thinking is certainly old-school in many areas. Nevertheless, I am equally as guilty of thinking I can obtain spiritual maturity my way and on my time line.

When it comes to cooking, I thoroughly enjoy it and do most of it from scratch. For those unfamiliar with the term "from scratch," it means I don't make a habit of opening a can, package, or freezer door when making my favorite dishes. I use things like flour, butter, and broth to make gravy, and tomatoes, veggies, spices, and meat to create pasta sauce. I enjoy making a wide variety of breads and have even been known to grind my own flour. This type of cooking is time-consuming and takes planning, but I am typically pleased with the outcome, and I believe those who eat with me appreciate my efforts. I have especially heard praise from those who are accustomed to picking up dinner from a drive-through or the grocery store freezer section. The difference between the taste of from-scratch food and quick food is noticeable. I find it interesting that my guests often comment that they could never cook that way, but after a brief discussion of some of my methods, they realize they *could* cook from scratch if they were willing to invest the time to plan and prepare the meal.

While many conveniences are associated with modern life, I believe there is also potential danger, in that our minds are being corrupted, and we believe we can accomplish all things immediately and with ease. For example, I have often heard one Christian express the desire to have the same type of walk with the Lord as another, more mature believer, but the less mature Christian quickly adds that this goal is impossible. The only difference between these two Christians is one's commitment to the hard work it takes to become more spiritually mature. Often we overlook the fact that the one who seems so well-grounded has been through some difficult circumstances to reach that point in his or her journey. We observers may not know of these hardships, but no doubt, they have occurred. Most endeavors require hard work for a person to enjoy results! This can be illustrated by the fact that one does not attain strong, healthy muscles or an appropriate weight without proper exercise and diet, although we wish it were not so. Advertisements constantly remind us that pills and surgeries can help us look our best. However, if we do our research, we realize surgery and pills are not the healthiest courses of action to obtain our optimum health. The same is true for our spiritual health and development. There is no "microwave" recipe, pill, or surgery to create the childlikeness we need so much.

However, it is beneficial over time to observe the walk of a mature Christian, as, regardless of our background, this would help us to learn more about the daily life we are on a quest to obtain. I have met many strong, committed followers of Jesus who did not come from a loving and nurturing home environment, but in asking about their lives, I have consistently found that at some point, they made a decision to accept the truth of God's Word, to become involved with a church body, and to carefully observe the lives of those around them to learn the proper, God-honoring way to relate to our heavenly Father and others. However, when watching others, we need to keep in mind that we are observing the results of life experiences that we may know nothing about, and not incorrectly assume that blessings simply have been abundant for some and not for others.

For example, while it was a blessing for Andy to enjoy a career in major-league baseball, it did not come without sacrifice, dedication, and many hours of physical effort and sweat. Also, Andy and I have enjoyed more than thirty years of an amazing marriage, which is satisfying in every respect. But we did not attain this blessing without working through some serious challenges. Now I have reached an age at which my children are grown, I have a solid idea of who I am and what God desires for me on a daily basis, and I enjoy a passionate and intimate relationship with my Lord and Savior, Jesus Christ. However, I accomplished none of this with ease. Instead, I reached this after experiencing physical and emotional pain, heartache, desperation, and loss—situations that anyone in her right mind would avoid if possible. We may not desire these experiences, but when we embrace and endure difficulties and suffering, the fruit will be sweet and nourishing to the spirit through the undesirable and unpleasant circumstances. The difference, once again, is attributed to our decision to walk through life holding the Father's hand.

To hold the Father's hand with freedom and confidence, we must look at what hinders our movement in that direction. We must look deep into our hearts and minds and begin to remove the weeds that have taken root and overgrown the childlike qualities God originally placed in us. We must be careful not to listen to the "voice" of those weeds. Yes, we can recognize the "voice" of the weeds growing in our souls, as it is screaming things like, "You aren't of value to God or the world," "You have ruined your chances with the choices you have made," and, "There is nothing good to find when you look inside yourself."

These are the lies of that destructive enemy, Satan, and plenty more lies are waiting for whoever chooses to listen to "the father of lies" (John 8:44). However, we are capable of kicking the impostor gardener out of the garden of our soul and opening the gate to welcome the strong presence of the master Gardener. Take this journey with openness to Him, the Father, who loves you, and listen carefully to what He says because the instruction, encouragement, and insight you receive are rooted in His truth.

Studying several of these childlike qualities may help us reclaim them as we understand how these traits became covered up or eliminated in the first place. While we use phrases such as "the faith of a child" commonly while speaking, they are not so commonly found in the reality of daily living. While the following chapters will not be an exhaustive study of all childlike traits, hopefully they will trigger our thought process in the right direction. Once we get started, the unearthing of long held and inaccurate assumptions about the Lord and ourselves will follow, and we can correct them as long as we continue on that path of seeking the Father wholeheartedly.

Exploring the essence of childlikeness can be like shining a flashlight into a dark alley. It may be a little frightening as you approach the unknown, but your senses will be calmed as the light illuminates the area and reveals no danger. Each trait discussed in the following pages is found in unblemished form in a newborn baby, and each of us began to digress immediately upon entering our imperfect world at birth. If we have reached a place where we are choosing to venture onward to reclaim what we have lost, then we must do it boldly and with courage because the dark places will be intimidating at times.

Every aspect of childlikeness we explore will ultimately bring us back to the same point of our acknowledging the effect our past experiences have had on us. If we desire to change, we must accept our heavenly Father's love and choose to love Him in return with all of our heart, soul, mind, and strength so we can love others in the same way. If we stop short of this goal at the onset, we will miss the mark. It is imperative that we remember we cannot accomplish this goal without the Lord, and His flashlight, involved in the process. While anything we attain apart from Him may prove to be beneficial for a time in relating to others, we still will not have attained the freedom, contentment, and deep peace and joy that are ours for the asking and can only be found in partnership with the Father as we commit to the task. The Bible is like the light that assures us in countless ways that the Father desires to lavish His abundant love on anyone who seeks Him in earnest. The amazing part is though we may not have a clue as to how to begin this journey, the Father assures us that it does not matter. We simply need to grab His hand and take a step onto the path, and the journey will begin.

# STUDY GUIDE

1. What "microwave recipes," shortcuts, or checklists for spiritual maturity are you tempted to follow?

2. What hardships have you faced that were or could have been beneficial to your spiritual growth? Explain how you did or did not allow your relationship with your heavenly Father to be a part of those experiences.

3. What lie are you tempted to believe from that "voice" of the weeds, Satan?

4. Read 1 John 1:1–10, and jot down the benefits of walking with the Father and letting His "flashlight" shine on our hearts.

# CHAPTER 5

# RUN AFTER CHILDLIKENESS

To get started on the journey, it would be a good idea to watch children on a playground and note their various behaviors as they interact with one another. Making a list of childlike traits is a good way to begin the journey toward behaving more like children in our interaction with our heavenly Father as adults. As we ponder the many characteristics of children, we can reflect on our past and begin to examine the reasons we changed. Perhaps the reckless words and actions of others hurt us, we made bad choices that had unpleasant consequences, or we scrutinized the lives of those around us and adjusted our character based on what we observed. As each situation is etched in our mind, it affects, either for the good or the not so good, our future relationships with God and other people.

We should consider many characteristics, and several of them I will discuss in the coming chapters. But for most of us, perhaps the trait that comes to mind first is a childlike faith. Unfortunately, I believe that for many people, the quest to understand childlikeness ends with this one trait. The term "childlike faith" is almost cliché in the Christian community and is often referred to in sermons. However, I do not believe that Jesus intended for us to stop our journey toward becoming as little children by merely delving into the reality and benefit of simple faith. I think of "faith" as a broad term that encompasses traits like trust and belief. I will discuss these valuable characteristics at length throughout this book, as these are no doubt important aspects of childlikeness that we need to incorporate into our lives.

However, we need to consider the many other childlike traits that we can reclaim and sharpen to achieve the goal of relating to our heavenly Father in a purer and more carefree fashion. Seeking only a renewed view of one's faith seems to be an incredibly risky shortcut in obedience to the command Jesus gave to His followers. This shortsighted response reminds me of the retort I sometimes received from my children when they were asked to do a chore, such as cleaning their rooms. One of them might ask, "What do you mean? My room isn't dirty!" I might respond by pointing out the pile of building blocks in the middle of the room and come back later, only to find that the blocks were the only things put away! Why? We often take shortcuts in obedience, especially when we do not have a clear understanding of the importance of the instructions. When Jesus issued the directive to "change and become like little children," I believe the list of traits He had in mind included such qualities as innocence, vulnerability, and dependence, along with the acquisition of a deeper faith.

An example of another childlike trait pertains to the way babies and toddlers are naturally teachable. People take in most of what they will learn in an entire lifetime in their first five years, so we can conclude that childhood provides fertile soil for learning. Young children often are eager to try new things, and they learn many skills by watching the people around them. They venture into the unknown with enthusiasm, which is why they need a responsible supervisor to keep them from danger.

Until young children have experiences that make them uncertain, they are moldable in much the same way as my favorite types of candles, the ones I can shape with my hands after they have been burning for a while. The wax is warm, soft, and pliable and moves easily under my touch. But with children, failure, criticism from an authority figure, and fear of physical or emotional pain can hinder their ability to be taught. In fact, I have heard experts say a child should learn to swim at an early age because it will come more naturally then. Experience has yet to teach him that there may be something to fear, so he does as instructed.

When I was in second grade, my parents made me take piano lessons, which I did for seven years. I received some excellent instruction, and had I applied myself more completely, I would have become quite proficient on the piano. Unfortunately, I did not take advantage of the opportunity because I had already formed my own idea of how I wanted to spend my afternoons—and it did not include daily practice. In addition, I was shy at that age and was not open to a dedicated piano teacher's stretching me in that area. My lack of both commitment to the process and courage to face criticism and failure hindered my ability to be taught.

The pride we may develop as we gain confidence in our own intellect and abilities may hinder our ability to retain a teachable spirit. Extreme self-reliance may overshadow or even overrun the teachable heart of a child. We must overcome these self-inflicted, unpleasant, and harmful past experiences and understand that God would be pleased to see His child become teachable once again.

Fear, a natural response when a person feels threatened, is another common childlike tendency that can hinder the ability to be taught. During fearful times, our heartbeat increases, the adrenaline is released, and all of our senses come to full alert. When a child is very young, he will cry or run to a person who makes him feel safe. We learn quickly whom we can trust to bring us comfort and whom we should avoid in times of fear. As we grow older, we also learn what is appropriate to fear and what is not dangerous. However, we still have those irrational fears that assail us when we least expect it to happen.

As a child, I always felt safer when at least one of my parents was at home. It isn't that a child-care provider or my brothers were untrustworthy; it was just that my mom and dad held my esteem, and I felt that because they were the authority figures in our home, they would know how to deal with anything I feared. I remember when my older brother and I were home from college one weekend, and my parents and younger brother were out of town.

As is known to happen in Florida, the National Weather Service alerted us to prepare for a direct hit from a hurricane. We had experienced this enough to know what to do, and we completed the job in plenty of time. We had the windows boarded up, emergency lighting available, and plenty of food and water in reserve. As far as I was concerned, the only thing missing was our parents! By that point in life, I certainly was aware that God was to be my protection in times of danger, but I honestly wanted a human authority figure at that moment.

Before I had even a slight grasp of God's omnipresence, the Lord and I had to go through many more fear-filled events. But the faithfulness I witnessed as a child in my parents helped to create the groundwork where God could plant that seed of trust in my heart. I can attest to the fact that the plant has grown fruit; however, it is one of the weaker areas of my garden. Through every fear-filled incident, God patiently walks with me, and He provides as much comfort and reassurance as I will allow Him to give to me. My job is to receive what He freely offers.

When Drew was about four years old, Andy took him to a secluded beach to fish. They were a ten-minute hike away from the car on a beautiful inlet with a tree-lined beach area. They had fished, enjoyed a picnic, and taken a nap in the shade, and then an unexpected thunderstorm came upon them. Andy knew it was unsafe to take shelter under the trees, and the path to the car took them there as well. He decided the safest thing to do was crouch low on the sand. I doubt Drew ever knew the fear Andy felt or the danger they were in as the storm passed because Drew was confident in his father's ability to keep him safe. The image of Andy's large body providing a canopy over that little boy that kept him warm and dry is securely engraved in my mind as a reminder of the refuge our heavenly Father is to us even when we do not perceive danger.

The list is endless of the many childlike traits we can explore while walking hand in hand with the Father through the gardens in our hearts. Hopefully, your mind is actively working, and your soul is seeking to have your hidden traits personally revealed by the One who is most acquainted with the weeds hindering their thriving. After you spend some time observing young children and note their childlikeness, prayerfully consider what needs to happen for you to become more like them. The chapters ahead hopefully will stir your curiosity and interest as other common traits are illustrated. After all, the rewards of relating to the Father in this childlike state are sure to be abundant!

# STUDY GUIDE

1. Begin to make a list of childlike traits. Add to the list as you progress through the study of this book and the Word of God. Put an asterisk by the three traits you need to reclaim most in order to interact more freely with your heavenly Father.

2. Read Psalm 131. Meditate on verse 2, and write down the ways you think it may pertain to the acquisition of a childlike character.

3. What kinds of things do you tend to put your hope in, rather than God?

CHAPTER 6

# RUN FOR
# TRUST

My father was a stickler for being on time, and ever since I became a teenager, I have been, too. When one of my friends got her driving permit before I did, while it was nice to be able to go places together, I soon realized that being punctual was not so important to her and decided to find other transportation when I needed to be on time. No real harm was done, and my response resolved the problem. I recall a more serious trust-related incident a little later in life when I made the mistake of taking a day trip with a person I didn't know well. When we were on our way and out of town, he took out a joint and offered to share it with me. I had never smoked pot and had no intention of doing so at that point, but I was stuck in the car with this guy for the rest of the day. Being the rule follower that I am, I was horrified at the thought of what could happen if a policeman were to pull us over, not to mention I was concerned for my safety if one did not. I lived through the day without getting arrested, and through the situation became wiser in the placement of my trust. However, while in college, once again I misplaced my trust when I met the younger brother of some close family friends, who was visiting home over the summer months. I found him interesting, and he behaved like a gentleman on the few dates we had enjoyed. When I returned to college in the fall, he invited me to visit him at his school over a weekend and promised to make appropriate arrangements for my stay. Because I didn't own a car, he picked me up, and we drove several hours to our destination. I was in for an unexpected and unpleasant surprise. It seems he thought I would be thrilled with the arrangement of a hotel room with him rather than a dorm room with the girls. Thankfully, he respected me and my wishes and took me home the next day when he realized his mistake. That was our last date, and once again I had learned a valuable lesson with relatively little harm done, except to my pride.

There are much worse experiences in life than these, but these illustrate how easily we can innocently misplace our trust and how quickly we can lose our ability to trust others in the future. At some level, we have all been lied to, taken advantage of, and used to serve someone else's purposes. One of the most tragic ways the loss of childlike trust occurs is through the atrocity of physical, emotional, and sexual abuse. Each time that trust is broken, the person naturally recoils from the pain, and weeds begin to tangle up the person's childlikeness.

Webster's *New World College Dictionary* defines "trust" as "firm belief or confidence in the honesty, integrity, reliability, justice, etc. of another person or thing; faith; reliance." It naturally follows that when that person or thing does not prove to be trustworthy, our firm belief or confidence in the person or thing is found wanting.

For example, we sit in chairs daily without checking for their reliability. But once a recliner I sat in at my mom's house almost flipped me over backward. I never sat in that chair again, except with great caution. Another example is I love olives, and I buy them pitted because I am able to consume them with more enjoyment. But one time I almost broke a tooth because an olive contained a pit. Now I squish or stick every olive I eat, checking for pits. These are just two of many examples of things we naturally trust until that trust is broken. In addition, we cross streets expecting traffic signals to work and people to look at them, and we board airplanes without checking out the planes or the pilots' credentials. We do countless things daily without the briefest consideration and have complete faith in the outcome . . . until an event occurs that makes us take pause. Then we become more thoughtful, or perhaps we avoid whatever offended altogether. Naturally, we recoil at pain and do everything in our power to not repeat whatever caused the pain.

When it comes to a break in trust with people, the pain is much deeper, and obviously, we are reluctant to expose ourselves to possibly getting hurt again. The method we use to protect ourselves is often dependent upon who broke our trust, how he or she broke it, and how many times we have tried to trust again, only to be disappointed. The mechanism for protection may range from a simple decision to a complicated process of keeping other people at a distance. Both extremes, and everything in between, are tactics to avoid the agonizing effects of broken trust. Sometimes we have this experience because we are ignorant or naive regarding whom we should trust, and when the outcome is uncomfortable or distressing, we learn a valuable lesson. Other times, the excruciating effects of broken trust have resulted from interaction with someone from whom we have every reason to expect integrity, such as a relative, a friend, a teacher, a scout leader, an employer, or a pastor. When a devastating situation like this occurs, we may need the assistance of a reliable and capable counselor to work through the rubble left in its wake. Even so, I believe we all should begin by considering some examples that may enable us to crack open the door of our understanding into our response to people who break our trust.

Take time to ponder personal experiences that resulted in broken trust, and consider your responses to those experiences. Many of us have asked, "Where was God when this happened to me?" And if we have been educated at all about the attributes of a good and loving God, we may go so far as to question God's trustworthiness because He is all-powerful and all-knowing. We actually may conclude that if we cannot trust God to protect us, then we can trust no one, and therefore, we must take care of ourselves. This thinking is dangerous, as it could disconnect us from God and other people. During these times, it is important to remember that we have control, and it is within our ability to reconnect with both God and others.

To move forward in restoring our childlike trust, we need to take steps to understand the answers to any questions we have asked but have yet to answer. By the way, there are no easy answers on that quiz, but the answers are within our grasp if we will only reach for them. Our loving heavenly Father may use a close friend, a pastor, a counselor, Bible study, and much more to give us insight as we earnestly seek the answers. As we go to the garden to let the weeding begin, it is important to recognize God's trustworthiness and choose to place our trust in Him.

Trusting God is the first step, and trusting His plan follows closely behind. At first glance, there may not seem to be a difference, but as we inspect them closer, we may see a distinction. However, we may not recognize the difference until we face a required step of faith that threatens to shake the stability of our lifestyle.

Abraham and Sarah, followers of God whose life accounts are found in the book of Genesis, are great examples of typical people whom God asked to trust Him in a very bold move that created a nomadic life for them. One definition of "nomad" is someone who has no permanent home. Living that way even temporarily presents unique challenges, and if someone desires to remain faithful to the Lord while facing these challenges, the person must begin with a commitment to trust Him and follow His plan.

I felt like a nomad when Andy was playing baseball, as that lifestyle required us to move frequently during spring training, the season, and the off-season. Sometimes an extra move was thrown in due to a trade—a decision that did not include input from the player or his wife. During this time, we often lived in temporary housing and traveled with our limited belongings. Furthermore, each move required us to become accustomed to new grocery stores, doctors, and churches. Even getting used to the people in a new area can be hard.

In that lifestyle, we had some things in common with Abraham and Sarah, described in Genesis beginning in chapter 12. They moved often due to God's call. They lived in tents, and each move took them to a new land where they were unfamiliar with the local customs, religions, and markets. The writer of Hebrews outlines Abraham's life in chapter 11 and correctly states that Abraham obeyed and went when God called him. He lived as an alien in foreign lands, looked forward to eternity with God, and passed God's test of faithfulness. In return, God blessed Abraham abundantly for his obedience to Him.

I am thankful that the nomadic life of baseball never required me to live in a tent or travel by foot into hostile territory. But many people today face unexpected and perhaps unwanted displacement that may be the result of a job change, marriage, or divorce. Other people, such as those in the military, may have to move into a hostile setting. Wherever we are led, the Lord only asks that we face the challenges of the day with the same confidence Abraham exhibited when he trusted God for direction, provision, and safety. It is worthwhile to note that he made the time to worship God along the way, which shines a light once again on the tender heart that God is looking for in each one of us.

Today, begin the healing process in this area of your heart by making a conscious decision to place your trust in God above all else. By taking that step of faith toward Him, we will be clearing out the rocks and rubble from the soil of our garden to make way for continued growth and new plantings. The master Gardener is on His hands and knees, getting dirty right beside the seeker who desires a well-tended garden and requests His help. Our trust in the Father is the foundational trait that will give us the strength, courage, and wisdom we need to weed the rest of the garden within our hearts and uncover the other traits that have been neglected or buried. Trust me.

# STUDY GUIDE

1. Who has broken your trust? Take time to think about the circumstances surrounding those events, and write them in a journal.

2. What has been your response to others and to God during the times when your trust has been broken?

3. Read Genesis 12:1–9, and write down your thoughts about Abram's choice to trust God.

4. Spend time reading through Psalm 119, and make notes about the outcome of learning and obeying the precepts of the Lord. How does this knowledge help us in learning how to trust the Lord?

# CHAPTER 7

# RUN AFTER VULNERABILITY

Have you ever loved another person deeply? I'm talking about that kind of love in which you have shared your innermost thoughts and feelings with complete assurance that you were safe in doing so. You have walked together through experiences that were most definitely once in a lifetime, perhaps holding hands through the agonizing days before the death of a beloved family member. You have done crazy things, like spontaneously running away from life together, even if just for a day at the beach or a few days in the mountains, because sometimes running away with someone you love is just the thing to do. You have cried so hard it hurts, but the one you loved held you, and it helped the pain subside. You have laughed so hard it became painful, and you don't know how life could be any better. You have loved without reserve and known that the love would last forever. Then life brings.about unexpected changes that you do not discuss, and ignoring the problem seems easier than facing it together. Thus, your relationship is altered, and the comfortable existence you once enjoyed begins to fade into the distance. Finally, you choose to leave the relationship for self-protection, or the one you love walks away without looking back.

In a moment like this, the temptation to shut others out is very real because our pain is so great and we may not think anyone else understands. Protecting ourselves from the ache becomes our primary goal, and because we often have a good idea of how we want to get that protection, we may close our minds to the input of others who are more objective. At a time like this, once again we are aware of the fierce battle between our flesh and our spirit. We desire to eliminate the pain, and it is natural to want to do that immediately. So we may put a kind of wall securely in place to keep from being hurt in that way again, or we may rush into a new relationship that effectively camouflages the pain.

How many times this has happened to us and who the offending parties have been determine the strength of that wall or the nature of the new relationship. Regardless, if we keep that wall in place or refuse to heal properly, we may never experience love as God intended love to be. To experience that, we must understand that it is impossible to love and be loved without becoming vulnerable. Perhaps that is why Jesus modeled this aspect of love relationships for us while He lived in this world. Jesus traveled throughout His three years of ministry with the twelve men whom He chose as disciples. He shared Himself completely and loved unconditionally as He taught them the principles of healthy relationships. Yet when the end of His life came, those men walked away from Him in His greatest hour of need. His closest friends betrayed, denied, and abandoned Him! Even so, I am confident that if Jesus had to do it all again, He would love in exactly the same way and make Himself completely vulnerable. This Author of love showed His children that the risk of being hurt is well worth the joy of experiencing true and abiding love.

Unfortunately, we are not so quick to take that risk. It seems that when we have experienced an unhealthy relationship and have been denied the rewards love can bring, we somehow lose our objectivity. Building a wall eliminates any risk, and we think we can live without becoming vulnerable to another person. Or we prematurely develop a new relationship, which is like planting annuals among overgrown and weed-infested perennials to make the area quickly attractive. This is only a temporary fix, as the weeds soon will overtake the new flowering plants. Therefore, on our quest toward childlikeness, we must be willing to unravel and uproot the offending weeds from our wounded hearts to make way for the beautiful new plants God desires to put there. If we seek the Father first and keep our hearts and minds open to His leading, He is able to prepare the gardens in our hearts appropriately for the next love relationship.

My husband is my best friend, and I am thankful to say we share mutual vulnerability. However, even after thirty years of marriage, we do not easily accomplish or maintain this. Many times I am still afraid to share my deepest thoughts. This is not so much a result of Andy's past responses to my vulnerability, but simply because I have been hurt in love relationships before. The people responsible for those injuries and when the offenses occurred are irrelevant. Suffice it to say that they made me acutely aware of the risk involved in sharing myself with another person.

With Andy, I make every effort to push past my apprehension and ignore that unhealthy weed in my heart that screams of danger. When I do this and get hurt, because my husband is human, I am able to refrain from putting a block in place in the wall. Instead, in those moments, I choose to remember his character and that he has shown his love for a very long time. I may put up a temporary and flimsy wall, because I am human, which I can easily tear down once Andy and I have had the opportunity to talk through the hurt. Part of being vulnerable is being willing to keep pride at bay and receive feedback from the loved one. I must consider the possibility that the sting I feel from Andy's response to me is rooted in my unwillingness to listen and not because he has carelessly trampled my garden.

I had a best girlfriend who shared this type of vulnerability with me for many years. We had countless soul-searching, heart-wrenching, and joy-filled moments as we experienced everything from marriage and birth to tragedy and even death. I knew I had a treasure of great value and believed we would share our amazing relationship throughout our lives. In that belief, I was very sadly mistaken.

The relationship I shared with my dear friend was founded on our mutual love for our Father God. In fact, we dreamed of the ways we may be able to serve our Lord together in a mission field close to both our hearts. We rejoiced together knowing that, although we were inadequate and inferior to the things of God, He would use each of us in His perfect time. We gave of our resources and ourselves without reserve and found great delight in praying for each other regularly. I reflect now on a time when she told me how blessed she felt when I poured out my deepest thoughts, feelings, fears, and concerns and how she hoped I felt the same blessing when she shared.

One of many clarifying moments in this friendship came in a rather unpleasant way. My friend became very ill, and I took her to the emergency room while leaving Andy to tend to the household. She was in considerable pain, and we held hands through the night, without concern for appearances, as the doctors determined the problem. I had a family at home and wondered, at times, if I should leave. But I couldn't do it. I could not walk away from the one I loved in this time of agonizing discomfort. In the aftermath, she told me she would have understood and smiled had I walked out the door. Then she acknowledged she would have been very sad and crying on the inside because it was important to her that I stay and hold her hand through the pain. That is a picture of vulnerability!

One advantage to vulnerability is the more of it we give, the more deeply we are connected to the person we give it to. The problem with vulnerability is the more of it we give, the more deeply we are able to be injured if something goes awry. I honestly have no idea what caused my friend to withdraw from the relationship, but I wonder if something happened that dumped powerful fertilizer on ignored weeds in the garden in her heart. Regardless of the reason, a wall was solidly established, which effectively kept me away.

In spite of the excruciating pain that I will always feel when I think of my friend, I must confess that I would not have that pain removed if it meant the loss of what I gained from her. As Alfred Lord Tennyson wrote, "'Tis better to have loved and lost than never to have loved at all." We hear the phrase often, but perhaps rarely stop to think of its meaning and the misery that accompanies the loss. But indeed, it is better to have loved because the sweetness of its fruit is indescribable and of tremendous value. However, loving again requires determination to allow the healing of our hearts at the hand of the Father and courage to risk our vulnerability again.

We need true courage when a family member has stepped on our vulnerability. Our tendency is to withdraw, but we have an inkling that retreat may not be the best course to take when it comes to family. A young couple, whom we will call Paul and Amanda, once shared an unfortunate incident that revealed their desire to earnestly seek the Father instead of alienating relatives who hurt them.

Paul and Amanda had been married several years when they bought their first home. When the day arrived for the closing, they had to write a check for more than they expected, and it depleted their bank account. Christmas was only a few weeks away, and they didn't have much money to buy the types of gifts for their families that they were accustomed to buying. As they pondered their predicament, they remembered with delight that their enjoyment of the holiday season did not depend upon the gifts they would give or receive, but upon the celebration surrounding the birth of Jesus.

Forfeiting the purchase of gifts for each other, Paul and Amanda carefully bought inexpensive, but meaningful, personal gifts for each loved one. They found wrapping and mailing the packages particularly pleasurable that year because of the time and energy they put into selecting each gift. Christmas morning was quiet and peaceful as they ate a leisurely breakfast together and contemplated the joy of the day. They were filled with thanksgiving for the gift of baby Jesus and were grateful for the financial hardship that led them to a deeper understanding of the meaning of Christmas.

Later that morning, their phone rang, and they raced to answer it with great anticipation of wishing a family member a very merry Christmas. However, Amanda's joyful spirit left her the minute she heard the angry voice on the other end of the line. Her parents did not appreciate the gifts she had sent to them. In fact, they were insulted. Furthermore, Amanda was told she and her husband were selfish and stingy for only thinking of themselves at Christmas.

The young couple cried together as they worked through their anger, hurt, and sadness. They had been sacrificial in their giving, only to be entirely misunderstood. As they remembered it was Christmas and that the day was meant for people to focus on Jesus, they were soothed from their emotional pain that resulted from the family encounter and found healing in the spiritual encounter with Jesus! While the sting of that offense was difficult to forget, Paul and Amanda made a conscious choice not to let it affect their family relationships. I don't know what happened in the years after, but I do know that on that Christmas day, this couple kept their gardens free of weeds.

Even through the pain, vulnerability—essential for true love to exist—can bring us great joy and contentment. When any love relationship has ended, we may feel afraid to open ourselves up to another person again. But we would be wise to let the Father work with us to uproot any resulting weeds in order to create healthy, fertile soil for a new relationship. This is especially true if the lost relationship was unhealthy in nature, because the last thing we need to do is complicate a new relationship by having a heart bound up by a tangled mess of wild plants. After all, the one place our vulnerable hearts are completely safe is in the hands of our heavenly Father. He has full knowledge of everything about us, and still He adores His children. A relationship with the Father is a great thing to turn to because it is the only relationship in which we are in no danger of being misunderstood, carelessly treated, or abandoned. Remember the beginning point of this journey? We must accept His love, choose to love Him in return, and understand that we cannot reach the endpoint without His help. Then, we can wholeheartedly place our trust in the Father's plan for the next step in the journey.

# STUDY GUIDE

1. After reading Matthew 26, list the ways the vulnerability Jesus had with His closest friends caused Him pain.

2. How has your vulnerability been treated with carelessness?

3. Read Isaiah 53:4–6, and write in your own words the meaning of the phrase "by his wounds we are healed." How does each person benefit from His willingness to be vulnerable all the way to His death?

4. If we believe Jesus' example of vulnerability is one we should follow, how does this look in our relationship with our heavenly Father and in our relationships with others?

## CHAPTER 8

# RUN AFTER DEPENDENCE

In the early years, my married life was unsettled and uncertain, and I constantly had to remind myself of Jesus' command to not worry. I resisted a great deal depending upon His hand in my affairs, even though I knew He was capable beyond my imagination. This struggle became very apparent to me the year our first child was born, more because of God's graciousness than my decision to trust Him. I have never forgotten the lessons I learned that year about dependence upon my Father.

When the year began, Andy had a contract to play winter baseball in Puerto Rico, which, of course, was during the off-season in the States. While we were there, I became pregnant and returned home for the holidays. Then we traveled from Florida to Arizona for spring training. Seven weeks later and nearly six months into my pregnancy, I traveled alone in my fully packed car to San Francisco for opening day with the Giants.

With three moves behind us, we sat at breakfast discussing our housing options. As I ate and dreamed, Andy ate and read the sports section of the Saturday newspaper. The paper reported that Andy was going to be traded to the Montreal Expos! When we learned of that, breakfast came to an abrupt halt and was replaced by indigestion. Within hours, Andy had boarded a plane to meet his new team on the road, while I stayed behind to arrange for our belongings to be moved to Montreal. Two days later, I was on my way to meet Andy in Texas for opening day and complete one more move before the birth of our baby.

For two months, I traveled with the team, as it was not scheduled to play at home, in Montreal, often in April and May. Then, we were finally there long enough to find a place to live and get settled. My nesting instinct kicked into high gear! I worked diligently and enthusiastically to properly prepare for the birth of our child. I was ten days overdue in late July when we received the news that Andy had been traded once again. I had Robin in Canada, and Andy left the next morning. I worked feverishly to get our daughter's birth documents in order, and when she was nine days old, we were on our way to meet my husband in Cincinnati. Two months later, we returned to Florida for a short respite, and several weeks later, we were on a plane back to Puerto Rico.

In each of these circumstances, I was tempted to rely on my natural organizational skills and tenacious spirit. Sometimes we may believe that doing things ourselves is best, as our experiences have proved that others will let us down. However, I survived the many moves that year by listening to the Father for direction, as well as accepting help from my mom, team wives, and new friends at church. I was reminded at every turn that God is perfectly capable of meeting my needs and willing to do so. I learned He is capable of giving me the strength I need while often using others to help in the process. My responsibility is to share my needs with Him and others, listen for His guidance, and receive the assistance He offers. I believe the Father enjoyed my struggle and efforts toward childlike dependence upon Him. Through seven moves and five obstetricians, life got dramatically easier when I was able to yield to the Lord and let Him worry about tomorrow.

When we are born into this world, we are completely dependent upon others for everything, including food, clothing, shelter, comfort, nurturing, and, of course, diaper changes. As we grow and mature and become independent and provide life's essentials for our loved ones and ourselves, it is incumbent upon us to figure out how to keep that childlike dependence upon the Lord.

From experience, we learn many things, and some of what we learn, including knowledge related to dependence, is in error. For example, babies need comfort and accept it when given to them. Then, sometime after our infancy, we learn we are to be brave and strong, and we begin to think, *I can handle this myself*, or worse, *I should handle it*. We may even decide that crying reflects our inability to "handle" our circumstances, and perhaps we take it so far as to interpret our feelings as a lack of faith. The church is full of people who don't want to appear "needy," so they choose to muddle through difficulties alone. The danger is eventually we may get to the point where we believe we don't need anybody—including God.

Certainly, we are to take care of ourselves responsibly as we grow up and become able to do so. But receiving some essentials in life requires the engagement of others. For example, the source of love, God, is intended to be shared with and through other people. Furthermore, many situations that affect us are out of our control, and sharing them with others potentially will lighten the load. If we are unwilling to share our needs because we have practiced our independence for too long, we have a good chance of missing the blessing God wants to provide! We have difficulty understanding that God has the ability to weave together our struggle with independence and the chaos of life in such a way that leaves us astounded. Perhaps dependence and responsibility have become tangled up in the gardens of our hearts, and we may need to spend some time figuring out the difference between the weeds and the good plants.

To meet us at our point of need, God often uses other people, but the balance comes as we grasp the concept that we must ultimately set the foundation of our lives upon Him. As responsible adults, we have relationships, jobs, homes, children, savings accounts, church activities, investments, and the list goes on. From these things and the people in our lives, we develop a sense of security, which is only appropriate when kept in check. The mind-set of the world certainly encourages us to run with fervor toward independence, and our natural tendencies rebel against dependence. If we're not careful, the weed of independence may creep into our garden when we rest too long or get too comfortable in what we have provided for ourselves, and ultimately this weed will alienate us from what we need most.

It did not always come naturally, but I have learned to have dependence on God. One of three children, but an only daughter, I loved being "Daddy's little girl," even into my adult life. My father loved the Lord with passion and consequently was able to love my mother and his family with the unconditional love we receive from our heavenly Father. My father gave of himself to the church, his work, and the community in such a way that he was loved by many. He was the one we went to for financial advice, theological understanding, and political discussions. He was a great debater, but he knew how much I hated to argue, so he engaged in less stressful conversation with me. He listened to me practice the piano, put cool rags on my forehead when I was sick, and gave me amazing hugs. I married a man very much like him.

When he was sixty and I was eight months pregnant with our youngest child, Joshua, my daddy collapsed with a brain tumor. My world seemed to collapse along with him. After the initial surgery, we learned the cancer was aggressive, and the realization that my father would not be alive much longer hit me incredibly hard. A couple of months before he passed away, I received a call from my husband, asking me to come pick him up at the doctor's office. When I asked him what was wrong with his car, he carefully explained that he needed to go directly to the hospital and was not permitted to drive because of a problem with his heart. Andy, who had been experiencing chest pains for several weeks, was trying to protect me from further pain. And I thought my foundation was shaken when Daddy became ill. It was really rocking now, and I desperately cried out to God, begging Him not to take both of my men from me at the same time.

At that point, I realized I had not solidly built my life upon the proper foundation. I had inadvertently settled into a comfortable place of letting my security rest on the people whom I loved and trusted the most, rather than on God. The transformation in my thinking and believing did not happen overnight, but that eye-opening experience was the beginning of my journey back to a firm dependence upon my heavenly Father. My daddy died, God spared my husband, and I grew up a little more that day. I grew up into a child as I reclaimed a small portion of a quality I was lacking. My journey continues as my spirit yearns for and seeks dependence upon the Father.

# STUDY GUIDE

1. How do you personally struggle in depending upon God to be your solid foundation in life?

2. Explain how you feel about verbally sharing your needs with God and with your close friends.

3. Can you think of an experience in which God has used another person or a group of people to meet you at your point of need? Explain.

4. Read 2 Corinthians 8:1–15. Write down what you see in the Scripture about how we are to relate to God with complete dependence.

# CHAPTER 9

# RUN WITH HONESTY

W e have heard the phrase "brutally honest" related to children because they say exactly what they are thinking. This can be refreshing or terrifying for parents because we aren't sure if the next words out of their mouths will be adorable or deplorable! For this reason, and many more, child-rearing was not meant to be done alone. But when this is necessary, it has been known to result in exhaustion and impatience. I have to admit that for me, those times became more common as the summer heat and the baseball schedule wore on each year.

While Andy was playing for the Montreal Expos, the sun set very late in the day and rose quite early in the morning during the longest days of summer. This was not helpful when it came to settling children into bed for a desirable long night's rest. Nor did the heat help me because most homes in Montreal did not have air conditioning, as the residents, who experienced extensive very cold winters, welcomed the heat. A further challenge presented itself to me in the form of two active and strong-willed children.

The summer that our first two children were ages one and three proved to be particularly difficult. The baby, Drew, was breastfed and high-energy; thus, he required my regular attention. Our daughter, Robin, proved to be an imaginative child who really liked to play. When bedtime came and Daddy was out of town, I was usually at the end of my supply of energy and patience, and my going up and down the steps of our townhouse didn't help matters. This was the case on the night of the cat incident.

Drew was asleep, and I was already thinking about my quiet night ahead with a good book. I prayed with Robin and tucked her in bed, only to find her at my side as I reached the bottom of the stairs. She was bubbling over with words, explaining that there was a cat in her room, but because I knew we did not own a cat, I walked her back to her bed, telling her that she had probably seen a shadow. After settling her a second time, I headed back downstairs, but once again Robin was right at my heels. This time, when she insisted the cat was now under her bed, I responded less patiently and rather forcefully, telling her that if she got out of bed again, I would have to punish her. Robin and I checked for any occupant under the bed before I gave her my best mom look and turned out the light. I gave up on going downstairs to unwind and decided to crash in my bedroom, down the hall. Before I reached my door, a cat scampered past me and took refuge under my bed. After capturing the stray cat and putting it outside, it was time for me to crawl to my three-year-old daughter's bedside and apologize. Robin looked at me with her beautiful big brown eyes and simply said, "I knew it was there, Mommy."

Though I had never seen that type of behavior in Robin before, I expected she was being dishonest to get out of going to sleep. I was so caught up in my personal concerns that I overlooked one of the most precious childlike qualities in her. The honesty about the cat and her shock at my disbelief were both valuable things for me to observe. This type of genuine transparency is beautiful in children—but sometimes lacking in adults.

As we grow and learn that it is acceptable to twist the truth just a little and call it a "white lie," our childlike honesty becomes buried. We also have witnessed adults telling a lie when it was convenient or when they didn't want to hurt someone's feelings. In fact, it seems telling a lie is easier to learn than telling the truth with tact and graciousness. Thus, we face the temptation to lie at some level every day. But not being honest with ourselves, God, and others is a dangerous path to take, as it unwittingly gives weeds fertile soil in which to grow in the gardens of our hearts.

The Bible explains that temptation is not from God; rather, it is enticement by our own desires. These enticements may be serious areas of sin in our lives or simply areas of naiveté yet to be noticed. In either case, they need to be recognized for what they are and addressed at the earliest possible moment. Temptation by itself is not a sin; what it can result in is another story. Therefore, it is important that we develop the habit of being honest with ourselves and taking any areas of concern to the Lord in prayer so we do not act on the temptation and enter into sin. At times, a discussion with a trusted friend may be necessary to finally rid ourselves of a temptation. Wrongdoing, or sin, enjoys the cover of darkness, and sharing it—or even the thought of it—with the Lord and a friend who will hold us accountable is a good tool for shining light on that dark place. I can personally attest to that.

During the baseball season road trips, I never got used to the time apart from my husband. In retrospect, I realize I was emotionally vulnerable due to my loneliness and lack of life experience. One summer in particular, this set of circumstances caused me some grief until I discovered the solution. In every city where we lived, one of my first orders of business was to find a church. I met friends across the country, with whom I am in contact to this day because of the relationships we formed. Often my friends invited me into their homes to share a meal or because they thoughtfully wanted to give me a break from my "single parenting." One summer I formed a particularly close connection with a family, as the family members included our children and me in most of their family activities. At some point, I realized my thoughts were drifting to the man of the house more often than was appropriate. It truly was not a sexual attraction but was probably rooted in the fact that he was home every night with his feet under the dinner table and his hands available to help out with the children. This unwanted emotion of mine puzzled me, as I was in no way unhappy in my marriage.

I could not figure out why my mind would wander in the direction of this other man.

So I spoke to a trusted Christian sister on the team and asked her for advice. She wisely said the only way to rid myself of these unwelcome thoughts was to throw them into the light by confessing them first to the Lord and then to my husband. I was mortified at the thought! Baring my soul before the Lord was not difficult for me because I trusted He knew my innermost feelings and therefore understood that I wanted nothing of this man besides his friendship. On the other hand, Andy is human, and I was concerned he would misunderstand the entire situation. I was more scared than I have ever been as I pondered my husband's possible reactions if I were to honestly share my struggle. My imagination ran wild, and at my very core, I wondered if we would still share the same level of trust after my confession.

A few days later, Andy returned home from his two-week road trip, and I had strategically planned an afternoon picnic for the two of us. While we ate, my insides were in turmoil, as the moment of pure honesty was fast approaching. When that moment arrived, I told Andy everything and expressed my sorrow for the hurt I may have caused him. I explained what the Lord had taught me about temptation and assured him that my love for him was stronger than ever. I finally finished . . . and was waiting for Andy to respond. At that moment, time stood still. Then, I was so relieved to hear him say he understood that I was only tempted and had not crossed the line with my actions. He said he appreciated my honesty! I had expended great amounts of energy worrying—all for nothing. My being open and honest with Andy created a greater level of trust between us. But the most amazing aspect of that experience was I became free of the temptation to sin as soon as I was honest with the Lord and my husband about the problem. When the temptation was thrown from the darkness into the light, it lost all power over me!

Because of the power deceit can wield, honesty is a trait that is difficult for us adults to cultivate, as the result is uncertain. There is always the glaring temptation to keep our sin under the cover of darkness. Reclaiming childlike honesty begins with the decision to let the light of truth shine in every area of our lives. We discover the real meaning of power as we become increasingly more comfortable in our honest interaction with our heavenly Father and with others. While training ourselves in the art of honesty, we must learn how to be tactful, rather than brutal, so we do not unnecessarily cause pain to another person. There is no question that the development of honesty in our everyday lives takes commitment and practice and will involve vulnerability and trust. However, if we can reclaim this quality, the hard work will be well worth it. And that's the truth.

# STUDY GUIDE

1. In which relationships do you struggle the most with being honest?

2. What do you fear about complete openness?

3. What can we learn about truth and deceit from studying Ephesians 4:17–32?

# CHAPTER 10

# RUN FOR INNOCENCE

As hard as it is for me to understand, my father enjoyed pulling weeds out of the yard. I have a mental image of him in the front yard, bending from the waist to extract a stray weed he saw in the lawn on his way in from the car after coming home from work one evening. He enjoyed the feel of the dirt in his hands, and I know a day's work in the yard was rewarding and brought him great joy. Even after I was married, I knew I could expect to see a healthy lawn with green hedges and flowers to brighten the view at my parents' home. Before our arrival one weekend, my parents had spent the afternoon planting pansies, and the front walk was absolutely beautiful with their splendor. Not long after our arrival, our three-year-old daughter and her little cousin decided to pick a bouquet for their grandma and plucked a handful of the pansies from that newly planted flowerbed. The memory of the look on my mother's face as she watched those two precious little girls enter the kitchen is priceless. I am happy to say that my mother was as gracious as ever, and it was many years before the children knew what they had done! I have remembered this story often when thinking about the topic of innocence. That's because those children's motive was simply to please their grandma with a special gift; there was no harmful intent. Their actions that day paint a perfect picture of innocence. We often observe young children behaving innocently and sigh as we comment about their sweet natures, even though their actions are not always pleasing.

Unfortunately, our innocence is lost in countless ways in childhood, as teenagers, and into adulthood. Attentive parents do all in their power to protect the minds of their children by avoiding certain environments, music, movies, and people. But because we don't live on a secluded island, we inevitably see, hear, and experience things that were not intended for us to be subjected to. When children have been exposed to something that puzzles them, they may ask questions as they try to reconcile the new information with beliefs they previously held. In some cases, children may keep an incident to themselves and draw their own conclusions, in which case weeds begin to sprout in the gardens of their hearts. The loss of innocence at some level is a normal part of the maturing process, but too much loss at the wrong time can lead to a hardness of the heart, and the connection to the innocent child within may be damaged. If, as adults, we are aware that these weeds exist and have been left unattended, our dealing with these wounds is essential. For those who desire help, resources are available.

When I was in high school, I experienced somewhat of a loss of innocence at my weekend job. I worked at a restaurant as a hostess. My hostess station was often in the upstairs section that overlooked the bar below, where a band would play. Because I have always enjoyed music, I found that particular location a pleasant place in which to pass the time on a slow night. The childlike innocence I possessed then I often expressed in a smile. As an adult,

I have come to understand that there are certain times to keep the smiles low-key. But my childlike innocence was still intact as I often listened to the band from that place upstairs. The leader of the band, a rather large man with a happy countenance, on one occasion seemed to relish the fact that I took such a keen interest in the music. When the band took a break, I was astonished to see him come up the spiral staircase in my direction. Because it was almost closing time, the upstairs was nearly empty, and this man took advantage of the dim lighting to conceal his next action. I was taken completely by surprise when he wrapped his arms around me, pulled me close, and proceeded to kiss and touch me in an inappropriate and offensive manner. When he realized my alarm and detected my rigid response, he quickly released me and left the area. I have no idea if he was misreading my smile or taking advantage of my innocence. But it doesn't matter; either way, my innocence had been affected.

As adults, maybe we have intentionally exposed ourselves to worldly pleasures that have destroyed our innocence, such as inappropriate sexual activity, pornography, or degrading movies or music. Perhaps we have been subjected to someone who shamelessly helped himself to our innocence. It is easy to lapse into the wrong assumption that the damage has been done so it really doesn't matter anymore and deny the weeds exist. But it does matter! We cannot erase our memories, but we can allow the master Gardener access to our hearts so He can uproot the ugly weeds and plant something beautiful in their place. We absolutely can reclaim our childlike innocence by submitting our thoughts, actions, and motives to the Father daily for His inspection. Asking God to forgive us for our sinful thoughts and behaviors might be a good place to begin. Next, as we invite Him to reveal to us the places where we continue to allow the mind-set of the world to taint our innocence, we have the responsibility of turning our thought life back toward the things of God, as Philippians 4:8 says: "Whatever is true, whatever is noble, whatever is right, whatever is pure, whatever is lovely, whatever is admirable—if anything is excellent or praiseworthy—think about such things." Our thoughts, actions, and motives are choices! We will need to pay close attention to the directions in which we allow our minds to go, use extreme discipline in reshaping the ways we act, and carefully consider the motives behind our choices. Deliberately selecting activities that expose us to the enjoyment of innocence may be a great second step. Some suggestions are to go with a child to see a G-rated movie, take stale bread to a pond and feed the ducks, or lie on a blanket in the backyard on a clear night and be amazed by the stars and moon. We will reap the benefit of nurturing these and beautiful new plants in the gardens of our hearts. As we retrain our minds and behavior, we will do much to reestablish our childlike innocence, and we will better understand the importance it holds in relating to our heavenly Father.

# STUDY GUIDE

1. How has your innocence been damaged by virtue of just living life in this world?

2. What choices have you made that ultimately led to a loss of innocence?

3. While you may not forget these incidents, what actions can you take to reclaim what has been lost?

4. Read, meditate on, and pray about the truths found in Psalm 103 and Philippians 4:4–9. Make a list of the truths found in these passages and the suggestions you find to reclaim your lost childlikeness.

# CHAPTER 11

# PRUNE THE OVERGROWTH

Growing a beautiful garden involves more than just fertilizing the plants and pulling the weeds. There also needs to be a time for pruning. During this process, the overgrown, unhealthy parts are cut off so the nutrients can be effectively dispersed. Pruning also enables the gardener, in his wisdom, to shape the plant for optimum beauty. In the same way, we may need pruning in areas of our hearts that have become overgrown, areas to which we may not have always allowed the Father access. Perhaps we have not allowed this out of ignorance or because the excess growth brought us security, validation, or comfort. It may be a combination of these, or for many other reasons. The important thing is that we contemplate the possibilities by once again becoming introspective and letting the light of God's truth shine in the hidden places of our souls, which we have protected for so long.

I'd like to share an example of an overgrown childlike trait in my own life. For most of my life, I have taken great comfort in learning the rules that govern my world and living responsibly within those rules to the best of my ability. For example, I vividly remember when I was five years old and entering a new school. My mom dropped me off in the gym, where all the children gathered before the bell rang, and I felt incredibly uncomfortable because I didn't know what was expected of me. When I was in school, I didn't talk in class, I raised my hand to address the teacher, and I stayed in line, as instructed. I would have been mortified if I had not completed and turned in an assignment on time. I respected my parents and obeyed their household rules fairly well. Now, as an adult, I typically obey the speed limit. When I enter a new environment, I observe the acceptable behavior and listen for instructions so I will be able to interact within the guidelines provided. Since I have been taught about God for my entire life and have chosen to follow Jesus since my preteen years, I have always been aware of the precepts of the Lord. Although I have faltered countless times, I have aimed to obey these teachings. A rule-following, law-abiding lifestyle has brought comfort to me, and I have been rewarded often for my obedience.

While at first this may not appear to be a negative trait, let me paint a picture of what was transpiring in my heart as it relates to the very responsible person I had become. Well into my adult life, I never missed attending church on Sunday unless I was deathly ill. Even then, I felt great guilt in missing corporate worship. I was rigid in my belief as to what a person should wear to church and felt uncomfortable in any worship setting that was unfamiliar to me. I said yes to every request for committee involvement in my church and in the community and even began support groups for people who had no place to share their specific life struggle.

At one point, I had a nursing infant and dying father yet still cooked the Wednesday night meals at our church for more than one hundred people—

until a wise elder "fired" me. I was stunned and hurt until he explained that I was spreading myself too thin and he was concerned for my well-being. I should have seen this warning sign, but I missed it completely! I was available to anyone who needed a listening ear and would carefully schedule an appointment with that person that would not interfere with my children's or husband's time with me. I ignored another warning sign in my mom's last year of life, when she often expressed her concern for my hectic schedule, as I spent an hour or two with her each evening after I tucked my children into bed. If you are reading this and wondering, *What's wrong with this picture?* then you also may have an overdeveloped responsibility plant in your garden!

In time, this overgrown trait began to strangle and choke the life out of me, literally, and I became physically unwell. The first time I became aware of the problem, it involved a hospital stay and several weeks of rest. Unfortunately, the plant was very deeply rooted, and its branches took control of my life. Thus, I did not realize those branches blocked my view of the Father. After all, what could possibly be wrong with living a responsible life? Within a year, I had returned to the same lifestyle. It was four more years before God alerted me to my problem again, and this time, I was forced to pay attention. My doctor warned me severely, and my husband came to the rescue by removing me from every responsibility I had outside of my family and job. During my weeks of recuperation, I realized I needed help to overcome this problem and sought out a trusted mental health counselor.

Then I came to understand that my responsible lifestyle had become a sort of "god" to me in that I had received encouragement and accolades from my family, friends, and those I served, which brought me deep satisfaction. My fulfillment in life was coming from the wrong source. It became clear to me that I was making up my own definition of a "responsible" lifestyle based on what I believed those in my circle expected of me. These "expectations" were not in the form of demands of others, but demands upon myself. By that, I mean I had taken notice of the acts of service in the lives of Christians around me and desired to pattern my life after them. I concluded that I had to do the things they were doing to live a life that pleased my heavenly Father. I had witnessed the impact of my parents' service in the lives of others as they worked in our church. Throughout our years in baseball, I had appreciated acts of service toward my family and me. I had traveled on mission trips to see firsthand how we are to share our testimony concerning Jesus Christ with others. So my definition of "responsible" came to incorporate being involved in the local church, opening my home to everyone who had a need, cooking for others in and out of my household, sharing the gospel in local and global missions, and being available *always* for anyone who wanted something of me. The word "no" was not in my vocabulary!

The biggest problem with all of this is I did not realize the toll it was taking on my body and my soul. My body had become worn out and unhealthy. My soul had become filled with the praise of people rather than of God!

To rid myself of the deeply rooted "responsibility" weed, I needed to learn that the most fulfilled Christian is the one who is serving in the way God has designed, prepared, and called him to serve! God has created no other person exactly like me, and no one has had the same experiences. This makes me uniquely qualified for the work my heavenly Father would have me accomplish with Him for the benefit of His kingdom. Before I launch myself into service, it is imperative that I acknowledge my usefulness and seek direction from God.

As this new plan played out in my life, I had to use words like "No" and "Let me pray about that first," rather than immediately responding to a request with, "Yes." I have to admit, this type of response felt incredibly irresponsible until I practiced it long enough to get the correct definition of "responsible" deeply rooted in my mind. Later, the healthier reply came much easier as I learned to discern the Father's will in my life. Now, receiving accolades is not my motivation, my goal, or my "god," but instead an added blessing and a source of encouragement. I desire to serve the One who is God, and as I submit to His plans more every day, I find that my fulfillment comes from knowing I am pleasing my Father.

When our family was vacationing in the mountains, we began to spend our Sunday morning worship time on the porch of the house overlooking God's beautiful display. The memory of our honest sharing, singing, and Bible reading brings joy to my heart, as I remember learning what true worship is all about. As our children reached their teen years and wanted to wear jeans to church, I was able to let go of my preconceived idea of appropriate church attire and allow them to wear what was comfortable, as long as it was clean, neat, and within the family parameters of modesty. I even began to allow myself to raise my hands in worship to express my love for my heavenly Father. I also learned to say no to others and myself and allowed my involvement to be filtered through my husband and the Lord. I was learning that I needed to relate to the Father in a much deeper way than following rules and checking them off my list.

Whether we consider man-made regulations or the valued statutes found in God's Word, we must be careful not to substitute a set of rules for a thriving relationship with the Father. When we take the expression of a precious childlike trait to the extreme, it can become harmful to our relationship with the Father. If left unchecked, it can even hinder our access to God or wall it off completely because the attribute has created overgrown hedges in the gardens of our hearts. I enjoy a walk in the woods, but I find it cumbersome to make my way through a thicket where vines and undergrowth are growing rampant. When that occurs, the walk is no longer enjoyable, and a feeling of oppression overtakes me. This is also the case with the overgrowth of our childlike traits.

As you can see, a relationship founded only on a set of rules cannot be fulfilling for either party. If I had given Andy a list on our wedding day of behaviors I thought would make me happy, and he exhibited those behaviors for the next ten years with excellence, would we necessarily experience a healthy, thriving relationship? If I had posted on our refrigerator a list of expectations of our children the day they were born, and they followed those instructions well, would we necessarily like and respect each other during the teenage years and beyond? No. That's because healthy relationships are founded not only on the principles that define them, but also on love. The desire to serve those with whom we are in relationship is a natural outcome of true love. The part that people often miss is that genuine love has its source in God alone. Any other attempt to love, from the flesh, or natural tendencies, may produce some desirable fruit but cannot produce the harvest the Father intends.

At times, most of us have attempted to take care of ourselves by running our lives our own way. After all, we are fully capable of surrounding ourselves with what we need to be comfortable and deciding what things we can be involved in that will create a rewarding life. Maybe we have had success in relationships with family and friends and therefore have either consciously or unconsciously allowed our childlikeness to be replaced by that self-reliance that gets in the way of our interaction with God. Perhaps we are overlooking the required beginning point of accepting a partnership with the Father. But if we stop to consider the end result, it is possible that we have worshiped the wrong god or gods, found comfort and satisfaction in those gods, and created a very heavy load to carry alone.

This was my experience early in our marriage. In our first year, one such learning experience for me began in making the moving arrangements upon leaving home for the season. Previously, my husband had been used to putting all of his belongings in the backseat and trunk of his car. But I used my wifely influence to convince him that I needed all my "things" to make our house a home, so we rented a small trailer to pull behind the car. My new husband objected several times as we loaded the trailer and made more comments in the unloading process. Mostly, however, he wisely kept quiet as I stood my ground, knowing he would like the end result.

As I set up our first small apartment, I found great enjoyment in putting away our dishes, placing our beautiful towels and linens in the hall closet, and hanging pictures on the walls. I had brought everything I thought we needed to be comfortable. The finished product was perfect, and I was content!

The problem came when Andy was called up to New York when the roster expanded in September. Not only would we not need our belongings, but also they certainly could not be checked onto the plane we boarded a few hours later. So everything was boxed up carefully and shipped home—at a great cost. That was the only year we enjoyed our wedding gifts before we bought our first home several years later. Therefore, the "things" that brought comfort and satisfaction at the onset proved to be a burden in the end.

The out-of-control growth of both our good and undesirable childlike qualities can become quite a load for us to carry around. Lugging that burden from one relationship to another can bring havoc into our lives like nothing else. But when we begin to expose all of these hidden overgrown traits to the loving hand of our Father, we will be on our way to freedom. With His light shining in the dark recesses of our hearts, we will begin to see the benefit of letting the Father be our garden Caretaker, who pulls and clips our overgrowth as He sees fit. We will not be as tempted to listen to or be intimidated by the lies of the imposter gardener. While the intentional and methodical pruning process at the hand of the master Gardener may be uncomfortable at times, we must cling to the knowledge that we have nothing to fear. The result inevitably will be that we are unencumbered and therefore free to let go of all the things we thought would bring us security and happiness. And we can rest in the only One who can truly be our refuge and joy!

# STUDY GUIDE

1. What are some positive traits that have become unsightly because they are "overgrown" in your life?

2. Describe a time when you may have gleaned too much satisfaction from what you were doing for God due to your many talents instead of giving Him the glory.

3. Read Romans 12:1–13, and then list some action steps you can take to develop balanced thinking in the area of using your talents and gifts to the glory of God.

# CHAPTER 12

# RUN WITH DETERMINATION

Even after we have taken time to consider the traits we need to acquire and are considering pruning the overgrowth of traits, it may be helpful to reflect on examples of people in the Bible who exhibited these positive traits. We can read the accounts of numerous people who lived in unusually difficult circumstances and through it all retained their childlikeness, as evidenced by their responses to God. They include Joseph, Moses, Samuel, David, a little slave girl, and Josiah. When we ponder the accounts of their backgrounds, we likely will conclude that, by today's standards, they were a messed-up group of people! Yet God was willing and able to use them in ways that brought blessings to them and eternal purpose to their lives. How was this possible? A childlike tenderness remained securely rooted in the gardens of their hearts regardless of the unfortunate environments in which they lived.

In the first book of the Bible, Genesis, we read about the early history of God's chosen people, the Israelites. In the lineage of this Hebrew nation, we find a young man named Joseph, who faced many of the challenges we also face in our dealings with family and power. He was the favorite child of a man who fathered twelve sons and was outwardly treated as such. Naturally, this did nothing to cultivate brotherly affection, and Joseph's brazen recounting of dreams in which he was the ruler over his family further enhanced the tension. When he was still a teenager, his brothers sold him into slavery, and Joseph was taken to Egypt. He earned a position of authority in the household in which he served, but when a woman falsely accused him of sexual assault, he was imprisoned. His merit was recognized again, and Joseph was made an overseer within the prison walls. After a royal official betrayed Joseph, he was finally exonerated and placed in a position that held the greatest power in the country, second only to the Pharaoh. God gave him knowledge and wisdom that prevented starvation in the kingdom, and later he was able to aid his starving family, which eventually paved the way to reconciliation with all of his relatives.

In the events of Joseph's life, we see ample opportunity for ugly weeds to develop, which would serve only to hinder a healthy heart toward God. While he may have struggled with some arrogance in his youth, he clearly overcame any haughtiness as he performed his duties as a humble servant. His master recognized that Joseph's obedience to his God brought him success with work; therefore, his master placed him in charge of all he owned. His brothers' selling him into slavery and his master's wrongfully throwing him into prison surely would have given Joseph every reason to become bitter. Yet, once again, he chose not to give fertile soil to weeds. Later, when Joseph got the opportunity to avenge himself against his brothers for their misdeed, he chose mercy and forgiveness instead. And although it was within his realm of power to cause them great harm, Joseph offered them grace in the form of food and expensive gifts to be taken back to their father. Later, the entire family moved to Egypt and enjoyed the fruit of Joseph's obedience to God. How differently this would have turned out for them all if Joseph had neglected the tending of the garden in his heart.

In the beginning of the Old Testament, in the books of Exodus through Deuteronomy, the life of Moses is described in great detail. The entire account sheds much light on God's character. But for the sake of this study, I will outline only the relevant portions. To recount his life in whirlwind fashion, he was born to Hebrew parents who were slaves of Pharaoh in Egypt. Out of fear for their child's life, they put him in a basket and floated him into the reeds at the bank of the Nile, where royalty was known to bathe. The daughter of Pharaoh found and adopted the child, and he was raised in a household of wealth and privilege, although his family had the opportunity to influence his understanding of the one true God in his formative years. When he was a young man, he observed the slave masters' treatment of the Hebrew people and was so appalled that he murdered the offender. Then, in fear for his life, he fled to a foreign country, where he settled into life as a shepherd, married, and produced children. While tending his sheep, he heard God's call to return to Egypt and act as the Lord's spokesman and demand that Pharaoh release the Hebrew nation from captivity. Moses raised objections to God based on his perceived personal limitations yet obediently followed the Almighty's instructions. He faithfully lived out his days in God's service but was not permitted to enter the land promised to his people because of a period of doubt and disobedience. The Bible proclaims at the end of the life of Moses that "since then, no prophet has risen in Israel like Moses, whom the Lord knew face to face, who did all those miraculous signs and wonders the Lord sent him to do in Egypt" (Deuteronomy 34:10–11).

Here we see a young man who was sent away from his lowly family home to be raised by foreigners who worshiped idols in the fortress of a mighty king. He would have experienced a life of luxury, with servants to do his bidding and any desire made available at his command. But Moses did not forget the God he was taught to serve in the earliest days of his childhood and, obviously, remained untainted by his lofty home life. He retained the tenderness of heart needed for him to hear the voice of God and to obediently yield to God's plan for his life.

Another child raised apart from his parents was Samuel, who became a great prophet of God. The account of his life appears in the book of 1 Samuel, but I will reflect on his childhood. He was born as a result of a mother's plea to God for a child, and upon his birth, she and her husband agreed he should be offered in service to the Lord. Though Samuel's mother cherished him, he was taken to live with Eli, the temple priest, just after he was weaned from his mother's breast. Perhaps Eli was a good man, but he did not exhibit qualities pleasing to God in the parenting of his two sons, which brought strong judgment upon them from the hand of the Lord. However, Samuel held fast to the laws of the faith that he had learned in the temple and grew up with a healthy, respectful fear of the Lord. Because he rejected the depravity around him and retained his innocence, Samuel was able to hear the voice of God when He called him in his youth. Like Moses, Samuel served God in a mighty way, and he was the prophet who anointed David king of Israel.

When Samuel anointed David, he was a young man. David's life story is described throughout much of the Old Testament, as he not only served as king for many years but also wrote many of the Psalms in the Bible. David's life was filled with much turmoil, although his early years were influenced strongly by the teachings of his father, Jesse, concerning the history of the Israelite nation and their relationship with the Lord their God. During the course of David's life, he was a fierce warrior with much success in battle, experienced great wealth as God blessed his kingdom, and accomplished amazing feats as he obediently listened to the voice of the Lord. However, he also committed adultery and murder and fathered children who did not follow the laws of their father's faith. Within his immediate family were offensive behaviors, such as incest, murder of siblings, and deceit.

Usually such horrible crimes are committed by the vilest of men who want nothing to do with a relationship with God. Yet the response given to those who objected to David's anointing at the onset reminded them and us that "man looks at the outward appearance, but the Lord looks at the heart" (1 Samuel 16:7). After David had committed these horrible acts, he becomes a broken man who humbly approaches God in utter repentance. Although David suffered consequences for the mistakes he made, the Bible describes David as a man after God's own heart! David had ample opportunity to grow arrogant and self-reliant with each victory on the battlefield. However, we see the continued nurturing and growth of the childlike qualities that enabled him to stay faithful to the Lord.

Early in the book of 2 Kings is a recounting I adore of one incident in the life of a little girl. She had been taken captive as a spoil of war and made a slave in the home of foreigners. Before her capture, she had been taught about God and had been aware of the miracles He had accomplished through the hand of His prophet Elisha. When her master, the commander of the king's army, became affected with leprosy, this young servant girl boldly and confidently told him he could be healed if he would seek the prophet of Israel. So the commander, Naaman, immediately sought permission from his king to go in search of this man. Naaman found Elisha and, after working through some pride of his own, followed the prophet's instructions and was healed of his leprosy.

This child was used as an instrument of God's and an example of faith. She exhibited innocence, sensitivity, trust, and an authentic belief in the God of her family. Because these traits were undamaged in her tender heart even as she lived as a slave, God was able to use this young girl. We might expect a bitter root to grow more quickly in an environment such as hers, yet this lowly slave girl remained childlike and continued to follow her God.

Later, in the book of 2 Kings, is some information concerning Josiah, who, like David, was anointed as king at an early age. He became king at age eight because his father was assassinated by his closest men. Unlike his father, who had been evil and permitted a rampant departure from the ways of God among his people, Josiah listened intently to the laws of the Lord when they were rediscovered and read aloud to him. He was open to the message found in the words, as his heart had remained teachable and trusting. Josiah decided to humble himself before the Lord and repent on behalf of his kingdom. In return, he was blessed abundantly in his lifetime.

The examples do not end with these, as the Bible shines a light on the lives of many who chose to protect and nurture the childlike qualities that draw a person closer to the heart of the Father. For instance, the book of Esther tells of a young, faithful Hebrew woman taken from her family to be part of the king's harem as he searched for a wife. Esther became queen and remained faithful to God even as she was later betrayed by one of the royal officials and nearly lost her life, along with her countrymen. Another example is in the book of Job, which describes a man who lost everything he had acquired in a life of faithfulness to God and chose to reject the advice of those near him. Instead, he held steadfast in his belief that the Lord had not abandoned him. And then, in the New Testament, we see young Joseph remain unwavering in his faith even when his betrothed wife, Mary, became pregnant with the Son of God. These people exhibited childlike trust, dependence, honesty, innocence, and vulnerability as they faced life's challenges with a teachable, pliable, and loving spirit toward God!

We not only have countless examples from the Bible, but we also can look around and observe people who have remained untainted by the tragedies this life can dole out. Perhaps we can provide personal testimony of an opportunity to nurture a garden full of anger, bitterness, and resentment due to undeserved harsh treatment in the course of life. Some life stories hold more dramatic tales of wrongful action than others, but the severity of the infliction is not the determining factor in the outcome. For every life severely affected by sin, resulting in a hardened heart toward the things of God, can be found a life in which a worse set of circumstances has been overcome, resulting in a healthy heart that is seeking the Father in wild abandon. Reaching the goal of reclaiming our childlikeness is dependent upon our earnest desire to immerse ourselves in the process with the Father in the lead.

# STUDY GUIDE

1. Write about a set of circumstances when you were more inclined to nurture your feelings of injustice rather than remaining untainted by life's tragedies.

2. List some examples of how you were tempted to harden your heart as a result of life's hardships. List some examples in which you were able to overcome that temptation. What made the difference in your response?

3. Read 2 Corinthians 1:1–14, and jot down some encouraging thoughts to remember during hard times.

# CHAPTER 13

# RUN OVER THE HURDLES

I have never seen a garden without weeds. Even the most well-tended botanical paradise has a weed here and there because weeds seem to grow as quickly as they are pulled. Naturally, the more hours spent weeding, the cleaner the outcome. Nevertheless, weeding will be an unending task.

So it is with our lives. As we learn by observing other people, if we take an honest look at ourselves, we will see that some undesirable fruit has grown in our lives. We all have tendencies and traits that need to be groomed and balanced, or even removed completely. These unhealthy behaviors may include gossiping, always wanting to "fix" other people, needing to be in control of every situation, being involved in excessive drama, and having eating disorders, to name a few. An unhealthy behavior may be mild or extreme, but either way, it may be mistaken as a positive attribute if another person is being well-fed by our undesirable fruit. For example, a gossip may be able to persuade others that she is not one, but simply cares deeply about the affairs of her friends, family members, and acquaintances. Then, someone hearing the gossip may feel a connection to the parties involved, and the flesh enjoys being included in such diversions. Similarly, others may regard a "fixer" as a selfless person who is always there in times of need. A person being "fixed" is relieved of the responsibility of carrying his own load, and his dependence is misplaced. The longer this behavior continues, the harder it will be for it to end because the "fixer" receives affirmation from onlookers, and the person being "fixed" is ill-equipped for life. This type of fruit may have been around for a long time without being noticed, but these traits are not desirable.

We must remember, no one is exempt from the effects of living in our flesh, so we must deal with our weeds. In so doing, it is incorrect for us to assume that exhibiting any of these traits makes someone a bad person. Furthermore, it is not a correct response to accept the behavior as a permanent part of one's character by saying, "It's just the way I am." We simply must continually groom our gardens in an effort to beautify them.

Once we have grabbed the Father's hand on this journey toward healthier gardens in our hearts, we will see our behavior follow along that same path. We will need to let the master Gardener show us what a weed looks like because we recognize Him as the expert in the grooming of the heart. Then we need to willingly let Him help us remove it. To propel us toward the recognition of our growing weeds and our need for assistance, let's ponder common phrases children say to their parents.

For example, when a toy was broken in our home, I can distinctly remember my children confidently stating, "Daddy will fix it!" Children say things like that because they believe mom or dad can fix everything. What about a child who is frightened by a storm, or at bedtime believes there is an alien in the closet or under the bed? A parental presence in the room brings comfort because children expect protection from all fears. Then one sibling who is attempting to control another may bring on the authoritative phrase "Mommy said so!" This statement ends the debate because the parent's final authority is recognized. "But I'm not tired" will be heard from the child who is too exhausted to make a rational decision and needs an adult to insist on the much-needed rest. Now think about the many phrases said *about* or *to* those in authority in childhood, and consider how it would be to freely say the same things about or to God. We find release when we relinquish authority to the master Gardener.

What a wonderful way to think about our approach to the Father when something needs to be fixed. Are we as confident as my children were that Daddy can fix it, and do we trust His decision about how to fix it? Let's look at the story of the widow and her sons in 2 Kings, chapter 4. She cries out to the prophet Elisha in her utter distress over the creditor who is coming to take her two boys as compensation for her deceased husband's debts. The woman is distraught over the thought of her sons being sold as slaves and has no means of obtaining the needed money. I cannot imagine she believed Elisha could give her the funds, but I believe she turned to him out of childlike faith in the God whom He served. Elisha asked what she owned of value, and she told him she had just a little oil. Then, he instructed her to go to all of the neighbors, collect empty jars, and then go into her house and pour oil into all the jars. As ridiculous as it may have sounded, she did as she was told, and when the last jar was filled, the oil stopped flowing. Elisha sent her out to sell the oil, pay the debt, and live on what was left. I am amazed anew every time I read about this widow.

When I put myself in this widow's place, I can imagine a time in my life when I would not have even considered asking for help because I couldn't imagine how the man of God *could* help. I may have considered my needs too great for an employee of the church to meet while forgetting for whom that man of God works! I also can imagine thinking his idea is crazy and more than a little humiliating, as I would have had to answer questions from the neighbors as to my need for all of the jars. I wonder if I would have gathered just a few and missed the abundance of the blessing altogether.

Like the widow, when we are afraid, do we run to Him first, and do we stand firmly on the conviction that God is the ultimate authority in our lives? I spent many hours in great fear during one summer of my life when our children were very small and we were living in a three-story townhouse. When Andy was out of town, I began to fear for our safety as never before. I kept letting my imagination wander to thoughts of someone breaking in at night and hurting the children or me. I would wake up in a cold sweat, and the adrenaline rush would keep me awake for hours. After suffering through many nights, I confessed my fear to one of the other wives who shared my Christian faith. She reminded me that God loves my children even more than I do and would most certainly be with us in any time of need. We studied some comforting words in the Bible, and I was relieved to be reminded of the truth found there. As a practical help, I would place my open Bible on the pillow next to me when I slept so I could read those passages again if I woke up at night frightened.

Also, do we listen to the nudge in our spirit when the Father is telling us to rest? I don't just mean the rest we get at night or a Sunday afternoon nap. I'm also referring to the encouragement we receive to slow down when we involve ourselves in too many activities. I was so hardheaded in my younger days that God had to push me off my merry-go-round to get my attention. I had four children involved in various activities and a family business to run with my husband, and I was enjoying many other interests, as Andy was now retired from baseball, and I got involved in community life. My neighbors joked with me about the number of times I went in and out of my driveway on a daily basis. Of course, I was too busy to recognize the many warnings the Lord sent my way.

Finally, my abrupt halt came with a four-day hospital stay. I was young and ignorant, but this did get my attention. It was strange to me that, although I was officially relieved of every responsibility, it took a while for my body to catch on to the new program. Much like when a person jumps off a fast-moving merry-go-round, my head and body felt like they were still spinning. The experience provided me with a better understanding of how to listen to the Father and the importance of paying attention to the nudge in the spirit.

When we decide to cultivate our gardens with the help of the Master, we will find that it must involve a commitment of our heart, soul, mind, and strength for maximum benefit. Then we are well on our way to the kind of relationship we were designed to have with the Father. We will be introspective, without concern for or embarrassment because of the weeds that will be found because we have accepted the truth that freedom from entanglement comes in our transparent approach. It follows that we will have a heartfelt desire to see what the Father sees and willingly work with Him to uproot those weeds that hinder our childlikeness. As we override our flesh inclination and seek the wisdom of the master Gardener, we will recognize the weeds and remove them. We will now be free to exhibit more of the behaviors we know are pleasing to Him. Then we can find comfort, knowing an abundant harvest of fruit that pleases God and the people with whom we associate each day will replace the undesirable fruit of our well-entrenched and unhealthy behaviors and beliefs.

# STUDY GUIDE

1. What are some of the habits you have allowed to form in your life that would be considered "weeds" in your heart?

2. What is your immediate response when you come up against an extremely difficult situation?

3. Read 1 Peter 1:13-2–5. What would you like your response to be?

CHAPTER 14

# RUN WITH THE RIGHT EQUIPMENT

If we have gleaned a clearer understanding of what we must change to redeem our childlike qualities, hopefully we are now ready to begin. If so, at this point, we must be willing to ask ourselves some pointed questions and to participate in deep soul-searching to find the answers. This will involve a consideration of our views concerning the Bible, prayer, the Holy Spirit, and fellow believers and may challenge or stretch our thinking as it relates to these topics. Each of these tools, required for the hard work ahead, plays an important role in tending the gardens of our hearts in our quest to redeem our childlikeness.

Before we discuss these tools, think about the tools used in gardening. A gardener must first prepare the soil. During this process, a hoe is used to loosen the soil to uproot rocks, weeds, or other unwanted elements in the soil. Then a rake is used to gather what has been uprooted so it can be cleared away, and the ground is made level. Then a shovel is used to dig holes to prepare for plantings. Fertilizer and water are used as needed to create the optimum environment for the plants to grow. The "tools" discussed in this chapter will be no different, as each will play a specific role in clearing out the assumptions, conclusions, and lies that we have allowed to dwell far too long in our souls. These tools also will enable the truth to take root and grow in our minds and hearts. And we will use all of the tools in conjunction with the master Gardener, our heavenly Father.

I want to stress again that it's imperative that we invite the Father to join us on this journey, for apart from His involvement, it would ultimately be a fruitless endeavor. We may begin the process on our own or perhaps with a trusted counselor, but the truth remains that God created us, and He is the only One who is cognizant of absolutely all that has transpired in our lives since our birth. Consequently, He is the only One who knows and understands us to the depths of our very being. Therefore, it makes sense that He should be our partner as we travel down this path toward a more thorough understanding of Him and ourselves. If we choose to include the Lord, we need to be mindful that we are involved in a personal relationship with someone who has never changed, will never change, and will never leave.

By definition, a relationship involves more than one entity, and certain principles govern them if we expect fulfillment. Communication between the parties and spending quality time together are two essentials. However, sometimes we may get wrapped up in our activities, concerns, and pursuits— which propels us into a self-focused lifestyle. Sometimes the routines of life, to which we have become so accustomed, create a barrier to our interaction with God and others. These patterns of behavior, with which we grow comfortable, are capable of leading us down a path that alienates us from those we love. This can occur in relationships with parents, children, spouses, and best friends, and if not corrected, may end badly for all concerned.

Relationships simply cannot remain on solid ground when one party is living a singular lifestyle. I appreciate the fact that God will shake up my life to get my attention if I am complacent for too long. Circumstances and needs change, and I can become so rigidly attached to my routines and schedules that I may fail to notice the changes. However, I am very thankful that the Father is always ready and waiting for me to turn around and invite Him back into my little world.

A situation with our daughter, Robin, really drove this point home. When she was four years old, she began to rebel against the concept of road trips. She made it clear, in a variety of ways, that she did not appreciate her daddy's leaving home every other week. She would begin to express her disapproval as soon as the suitcase came out of the closet.

Her dislike for this aspect of baseball was never more apparent than a day late in the summer when her daddy was leaving on a two-week trip. We said our good-byes at home, but Robin was sulking and refused to acknowledge Andy even as he walked out the front door. As he drove away, she went to the screen door and cried as if she would never see him again. My efforts to console her were fruitless. As the afternoon progressed and bedtime was upon us, Robin would have nothing to do with me, except to allow me to meet her basic needs. My heart broke a little that day as my precious girl chose to suffer alone.

The next day dawned with a better attitude, and the two weeks were fairly uneventful. However, our child's wrath emerged once again when her daddy returned home. During his first day home, Robin rejected her father's hugs, kisses, and words of love. With determination, Andy continued his overtures, and within twenty-four hours, our daughter chose to receive his expressions of love once again.

This developmental stage in Robin's life passed quickly, but the life lesson has remained in my heart and mind. Our heavenly Father always desires to be in close communion with His children. Our Lord wants to share every aspect of life with us, but we must permit His entrance. It breaks His heart each time we choose to suffer alone, and He is saddened when we neglect or forget to include Him in our everyday lives.

The Bible, prayer, and other people are all methods of communication between us and our heavenly Father. Each of these tools is most effective when we have received the gift of the Holy Spirit and our spirit freely communes with His. This is not to say that a person cannot gain some measure of insight by reading the Bible or that God does not hear the prayers of someone who is seeking Him but has yet to enter into a relationship with Him. Furthermore, people in and out of the church may be able to provide good advice for living. But attempting to use these tools without a connection to their Power Source would be very much like using a chainsaw without gas. His Spirit's living within us gives us the ability to hear from the Father through the written Word, during our quiet reflections in His presence, and from other people who share the faith. Furthermore, we can be assured that any direction or inspiration we receive He has tailored just for us because He knows us so perfectly. Finally, because all information has been filtered for imperfections through Him, we can be sure that we are hearing His message in its purest form.

## The Bible: God's Word for Daily Living

On the day I first set foot into a major-league baseball park, God provided me some experiential knowledge to remind me of the importance of asking for help from the correct source. This lesson occurred after the Yankees called my husband to New York during our first year of marriage. We went directly to the stadium from the airport and arrived several hours before game time. I was a little concerned that, in his excitement, Andy might forget I needed a seat. So the last thing I said to him was, "Don't forget to put me on the pass list."

I took a seat in the empty stadium and enjoyed watching the team practice while I daydreamed about the exciting days ahead. But when the gates opened, I quickly realized the need to find my seat, as a sold-out crowd was expected. There was a ticket window inside the stadium at the pass gate, and I gave my name to the attendant. She scanned the list and told me there was no ticket left under that name. I carefully spelled my name and had her recheck the list, but she still did not find my ticket. Thankfully, I was inside the stadium, and the team was still on the field, so I raced down the stairs to find Andy. While he was nowhere in sight, another player offered to relay my desperate message to him. He returned to say that Andy had definitely put my name on the list. Returning to the ticket window with confidence did no good, as the attendant still did not find my name.

Alone in a sold-out Yankee Stadium may sound like a contradiction. But I was young, inexperienced, frightened . . . and very much alone. So I did what my parents taught me to do in such a situation. I found a policeman who looked like a grandpa, and after I explained my predicament to him, he put his arm around me and spoke words of reassurance. He took me to the wives lounge and introduced me to the only person in the room. To my astonishment, later I discovered that this lovely woman sitting quietly with a book before game time was a Christian! She invited me to sit with her during the game, and though I stepped into unknown territory, I gladly accepted the offer. Whether she knew it or not, I believe she was in that place at that time by divine appointment!

I found myself lost, alone, and scared, but I remembered what I had been taught, chose to ask for help, and believed the officer had an answer. I also found I had received much more than I had expected. Not only did I have a seat for the game, but I was also in the company of a fellow believer during a time when I needed that most.

One necessary source of help in our walk toward change is the Holy Bible. It's not just a good luck charm, a collection of life verses, or a touching decoration for the side table in the living room. It is a source of help in times of need, a detailed account of the God we seek, and a way for our Father to reveal important, life-altering truths to us right where we are at any given moment.

The problem we may face is we do not immediately turn to this source of help, even though we may have been taught of its value. Perhaps we struggle with the belief that it is trustworthy, doubt our ability to understand its meaning, or feel intimidated by the authority it represents. Maybe we just failed to get into the habit of opening the Bible for assistance. Whatever the reason for our hesitation, the help is available to the seeker.

When we make it a habit to turn to the correct source for direction, we are never disappointed, and if we are willing to take the risk, we will get more than we are seeking. Many of us own a Bible and keep it on a shelf to pick up on the way out the door to church. We don't always treat it as the valuable tool that it is intended to be and simply think of it as a good book to read during devotions each day.

However, what we may be missing is that it is "living and active" and will enable us to recognize, uncover, and deal with the events of our past that have masked our childlike qualities. The Bible promises to serve as a light to illuminate the dark places of our soul as we lay ourselves bare before our Father in heaven. Then we must allow His words to probe into the deep recesses of our being to help us identify the source of our pain. We find words of comfort that give us the courage to relinquish that pain into the Father's capable hands, while the truth found in the Bible brings about a gentle healing. With each step in this direction with the Father, we find that our concealed childlikeness is free to flourish in the light of the Word.

The Bible is also a source of nourishment for our ongoing growth process. Just as we must make healthy food choices for our physical well-being, we also must make healthy choices when it comes to nourishing our souls. Unfortunately, we are prone to wanting junk food! My children were notorious for coming into the kitchen prior to dinner and asking for a snack. Even if a wholesome food was offered, they seemed to complain often and request a cookie instead. But their interest in a snack mysteriously disappeared once they realized that sugar was not an option. As an adult, I have been through periods in which I have indulged in a careless diet, and the result was excess pounds, low energy, and general frustration. Similarly, inadequate sustenance can adversely affect the spiritual aspect of our nature. We may be tempted to believe that reading a devotional in the morning or a spiritual book in the afternoon will suffice. But it is vital to our spiritual health that we fill ourselves to capacity with the truths in the Bible on a regular basis, rather than settling for a few snacks along the way! When we do this, we are able to gain confidence in responding to the world's expectations and demands as well as to Satan, who is relentless and merciless in his attacks.

The Bible is also a guide for our future as we seek to discover more about the character of God and apply that understanding to all relationships. As David's Psalm 19 states, God's Word has the power to revive the soul, make us wise, give joy to our hearts, and bring the light of understanding to our eyes (vv. 7–8). The key is to remember where to turn and use this incredible source of help in our time of need as well as the times when life is sailing by smoothly.

Many people have shared with me that they feel incapable and inadequate when it comes to reading and understanding the Bible on their own. This saddens me because I believe they are usually incorrect. If we are able to read and reason, we can benefit from a time of personal Bible study. Remember, we are not on this journey alone, but with our heavenly Father, who has the ability to give the reader insight. Our responsibility is to set aside time to read, meditate, memorize, and talk to God and others about what we are learning. We will quickly discover the benefit of doing these things as we experience a deeper connection to our heavenly Father.

## Prayer: Talking to God

When I was young and first learning about prayer, I paid close attention to how other people prayed. My parents prayed out loud during family gatherings, and as we grew older, we were encouraged to do the same. I listened to how the preacher and my youth pastor talked to God, and I developed the habit of praying to God in a personal way. In my early teen years, I found a prayer in the newspaper that interested me because it outlined the things I desired for my life and was similar to prayers I had heard from people I respected. I cut the prayer out and used it throughout my teen years as a model of how to pray. I faithfully asked my heavenly Father for what I really wanted out of life as it was articulated in that printed prayer. In my innocence, I had no idea what would be required experientially to attain such fruit in my life, but if I had been aware, there are a few qualities I may have left off the list. Nonetheless, I prayed the prayer with a sincere, tender, and open heart toward God. As I married and moved away, I packed away the clipping and did not rediscover it until my children were almost grown. At that time, I read the familiar words again, and they brought tears to my eyes because I realized God had answered the prayer of my little girl heart in abundance! I had held tight to the loving hand of the Father through the trials of life, and He had gently stretched, molded, trimmed, and shaped me during the times when I was mushy and pliable due to the hardships I faced.

When I was not so willing to allow His hand to form me, the Father waited patiently for me to come back into His embrace. Unfortunately, in spite of my understanding when it comes to interacting with the Father in prayer, I oftentimes get lazy in this aspect of my relationship with Him and begin to go about my life on my own. While I don't consciously reject God, I do inadvertently place Him somewhere other than the top of my priority list. I cruise along in life and enjoy the scenery because I believe I have it all under control.

It reminds me of the times when life as the wife of a professional athlete was exciting and provided abundant opportunity to see different areas of the country. In my travels by car, I particularly enjoyed the glorious views when driving through the mountains. Seeing trees, wildlife, and rolling hills is relaxing and fills me with a sense of peace and well-being.

Then I would see a sign indicating a sharp curve in the road ahead. Especially when unfamiliar with the area, I would slow down and drive more cautiously. As I would follow the bend in the road, I often would discover another spectacular view around the corner, whereas other times I would come upon road construction or bad weather.

Like on the mountains, sometimes in life everything is rolling along beautifully, and then life throws us a curve. Our satisfaction and contentment vanish as we struggle to put a new plan in place. In baseball life, this curve might come in the form of a trade midway through the season or an injury that threatens to end Andy's career in baseball. But for all of us, life is full of unexpected and undesired events, such as longstanding poor health or pain, broken relationships, financial ruin, a friend's betrayal, or the death of someone we hold dear. Perhaps we must face a child's illness or death, infidelity, an unexpected pregnancy, or a teenager's rebellion. My tendency is to figure it all out at the earliest possible moment, which frequently means I move ahead on the course that looks best to me without consulting the Lord in prayer.

Through experience doing things my way first when facing a sharp curve in life, I have learned that the best action I can take is to slow down or, better yet, stop completely. The perspective I gain is amazing, and then I become mindful to pray and seek the Lord's guidance for the new plan. When I choose to turn to God for the next step, a sense of peace returns. When I allow my heavenly Father to lead me around that "bend in the road," the view truly is spectacular because He is there to help me see my way through!

That is because our God cares about our every need before we even know we have it, a concept that is both baffling and thrilling. And while it is true that He is omniscient, He still desires that we turn to Him and verbalize our thoughts and feelings. While the Bible enables us to learn about God and His character, if that is the only way we ever communicate with the Lord, we soon would realize that the relationship was one-sided. We need to talk to Him as well.

Some people are intimidated by the word "prayer," but it simply involves acknowledging and praising Him as the one true God, confessing to Him where we struggle with doing the right thing, thanking Him for His existence and accessibility, and asking Him for what we believe is needed. When we first begin to communicate with God through prayer, perhaps we will find it is a little self-focused. But if we are sincere in our childlike talks with Him, God understands and appreciates our vulnerability, honesty, and openness.

God knows and understands our tendencies to focus on ourselves, so, as He is prone to do, He provides a way to help us remember our relationship with Him. Jesus spent the last hours before His crucifixion with those closest to Him and spent much of that time reminding them of the promised Holy Spirit that would come to them after His death, burial, and resurrection. Because this is a spiritual relationship, it can only be understood in the spirit, so when we choose to live by the flesh, we cannot really grasp this concept. However, Jesus told His followers He would return to be with them forever in spiritual form so that as His Spirit interacts with our spirit, He would be able to convict us of wrongdoing, give us counsel and guidance in the truth, and provide us with comfort and peace that cannot ever be taken away.

The Holy Spirit is able to remind us of those for whom we need to be praying. For instance, we may have an unexpected thought of a particular person in a day and realize it is the prompting of the Holy Spirit to pray for that person. Perhaps we are grieving for a severed relationship, and we are prompted in our spirit to let that grief remind us to pray for the one we love. Maybe we spend a day fasting, and the Holy Spirit uses our weakened hungry state to keep our attention focused on a specific prayer need. Or perhaps we are devastated by a tragedy, and the precious Holy Spirit—which is one with our spirit—consoles us beyond our comprehension.

Prayer is a spiritual interaction with God and a tool that is available to all who seek the Father. So we could experience the optimum two-way communication in this relationship, Jesus sent us His Holy Spirit. He is able to "speak" to us in a variety of situations, such as while we are reading the Bible alone, sitting in a Bible study, sharing life with a friend, talking to Him in prayer, or sitting quietly and listening for His voice. What is key is that we choose to have a relationship with Him and expect to hear from Him.

## The Church and Accountability

The quest we are on to reclaim and redevelop our childlike traits is an extensive and exhausting one but will certainly be full of rewards along the way. Once we get started, we quickly realize it is truly a journey that should never end. We may be on a crash course at first as we seek to grasp exactly where we need to begin in this personal trek, but regardless, like any challenging endeavor, we should include others as we travel this path to childlikeness. At times, we will need instruction or encouragement, and sometimes we will just need someone to laugh or cry with us. Other times, we will have material needs. At times such as these, God designed the church family to lend support in the area of need.

For us, baseball life was full of change. But for me, as a Christian, one thing that stayed constant in my life during that time was my relationship with Jesus Christ. Therefore, one of the first things I did when settling in a new city was find a solid Bible-teaching church. Sometimes I visited several before deciding on a church "home." Even though my husband could not attend with me, I knew I needed a church family.

In my searches, my experiences varied. I tried different denominations and consequently was challenged to seek the truth in God's Word for myself. It has been a great benefit over the years to have had different worship experiences that constantly challenged my theology. Also, I found friends whom the Lord used to meet the wide range of needs I had during that period of my life. Furthermore, mature Christian women mentored me. They helped me to learn valuable lessons about marriage, child-rearing, and living in this world. While I wasn't able to serve in the traditional fashion during those years, such as by working in the nursery or teaching a class, God did allow opportunities for me to be an encouragement to my fellow believers. With each church family, I developed valuable relationships with my brothers and sisters who encouraged me in the faith, and with each move, I left behind a trail of Christian friends.

The value of those relationships far outweighed any fear I experienced upon visiting a new church. God designed us to fellowship with other believers, and it is very important to do so in our pursuit of the childlike character. Since Andy's baseball career ended, God has confirmed the need for other believers in my life.

Upon Andy's retirement, we began to visit new churches in the town where we would be settling to raise our children. We had been attending the same church for about two months when I faced a tragedy. My mom called me early one Sunday morning and said my dad had suffered a seizure and doctors had found a massive brain tumor that required immediate surgery. Andy and I booked a flight to Atlanta for later in the day, and I thought I had my emotions under control, so we headed to church. But when a dear friend asked how I was doing and demonstrated genuine compassion for my situation, I fell into her arms, and she held me as I cried in deep anguish. Once in Atlanta, we stayed with my parents for a few weeks as Dad recovered from surgery. A couple of weeks into that visit, our home church pastor called to see how we were doing. He prayed with us over the phone and assured us that they would be keeping us close in their thoughts and prayers in the coming weeks. I realized that day that we had found a church that understood how to be a family.

For many people, simply finding a church to become a part of can be a daunting task. In this one undertaking, they may come up against all of their personal challenges to regain childlikeness. Becoming involved with a body of believers is like gaining another family; perhaps you can relate to how complicated that can be. In fact, that is the very reason you may avoid taking this step in your life. You may find it difficult to trust the pastor and elders because someone in a leadership position has hurt you. You may be reluctant to be vulnerable in a small group because you have been betrayed in such relationships. Or maybe you just don't want anyone to get close enough to really know you. If you have an aversion, you may need to consider whether it is to the concept of church, to Jesus Christ and His teachings, or to the thought of being hurt again. Our fear over finding a church family may be rooted in our past church experiences that were unpleasant, confusing, or both.

Contrary to what we may have been taught, what we have come to believe, or what the culture tells us, the church is not made up of perfect people or people who think they are perfect. Oh, you will come across a few of those, but don't worry; God will straighten them out. A good thing to recognize is the church is made up of people like us who make mistakes and may have wrong motives. Some people at church may even be deceitful, manipulative, and predatory. Also, we certainly need to be careful that what is being taught in the church is what we believe the Bible to say because even a well-meaning leader can get some things wrong when it comes to relating to God in a healthy manner and correctly interpreting the Bible. But as I would not avoid all restaurants forever after receiving bad service or a bad meal once, we should not give up on searching for a church because there are no perfect churches. We simply need to select carefully the group of believers we will call family.

In every church, we may come across untried or inexperienced Christians who equate a healthy walk with the Lord with a sinless life. We must be careful not to fall into this mental trap because at times, even the most committed follower of Jesus will exude a sinful thought, word, or action. The only perfect person who ever walked this earth was Jesus Christ! So if we set our goal as perfection, we surely will be disappointed and disillusioned because it cannot be attained. Rather, I believe the goal for each of us is to reach a point where we quickly recognize a sin in our lives because we are acutely in tune with the Holy Spirit and are committed to turning away from any sin He brings to our attention. When searching for a church family, it may be helpful to look for those who speak and live out that truth.

If we listen to the wrong voice, we will become aware of countless reasons to avoid getting involved in a church community. The wrong voice would be the one belonging to our natural self, the one that wants to avoid the risk of pain of any kind, at any cost. Or it would be the voice of that imposter gardener, Satan, who is trying to persuade us that we do not need a group of hypocrites telling us how to live. If we listen to either voice, the unfortunate consequence is we miss the good things that come from belonging to a healthy body of believers. Instead, we must step out and accept the risks. If we have an unpleasant experience, we should find another church that teaches the truth of the Bible and encourages its members to live it in their daily lives! The simple truth is the only way a church becomes a better representation of God's love is by each person in the church becoming a better representative. As we seek the Father and become transformed by that relationship, the church likewise will be transformed.

Before you decide on a home church, it may be helpful to understand the nature of the early church following the crucifixion, burial, and resurrection of Jesus Christ. The Jesus followers of that day gathered in homes, and because they were in danger of persecution, no one attended those meetings because it would look good on a résumé or so they could network with the right people in town. The message of Jesus was shared verbally, and participants followed Jesus' example and command to partake in the breaking of bread, or Communion. Also, those present offered one another much-needed support and encouragement. If a person was new in town and wanted to attend the meetings, he or she simply had to ask, "Where does the church meet?" to be given directions to the meeting place because there were no denominations established. Of course, some groups were harder to find, as they met secretly to avoid persecution, but the important point is to clearly understand the purpose for meeting. The early church shared spiritual instruction, worship, emotional support, and material needs. As we seek a group to associate with for these purposes, it may be complicated and likely will require all of the discernment we can muster. Prayer, common sense, and a listening ear to hear the voice of the Lord will be good tools to use in this process.

While a church family can be a great place for us to be nurtured in our growth, our need for others does not end with that group of people. I believe it is essential that we develop relationships with those who have shown themselves to have integrity and connect with them on a deeper level. The reason is sometimes God uses others to speak His truth into our lives, and we will not be available to hear the message unless we have cultivated friendships with these people. In this type of relationship, we must be able to trust, be vulnerable, and share our daily lives in complete honesty. It is important for each person in the relationship to give permission to ask hard questions of him or her and to commit to answering those probing questions. This kind of personal accountability can be of great and lasting value in the growth process, but should be entered into with great prayerful consideration of the friendship.

Even in the best of circumstances with an accountability friendship, we may struggle at times with speaking the truth about our observations concerning our friend's lifestyle or behavior. We may feel we have no right to shine a light on the person's sin, as we are guilty of sin ourselves and may have even previously participated in the behavior we now recognize as sin in our friend. The key is to follow the command Jesus gave to His followers to "first take the plank out of your own eye, and then you will see clearly to remove the speck from your brother's eye" (Matthew 7:5). Jesus never said to leave the speck in your friend's eye alone because you have no right to notice or touch it. What he said quite clearly is that we are to humbly search our own hearts, minds, and lives for sin, and with that taken care of in the sight of the Lord, help our friend do the same in his own life. The lie we oftentimes accept is that to point out sinful behavior in someone else is to judge that person. The Bible does not instruct or permit us to pass judgment concerning someone's eternal destiny, as that judgment is left to God, as He is the only One who knows the thoughts, motives, and all related experiences of each one of His children. The Bible reminds us that "man looks at the outward appearance, but the LORD looks at the heart" (1 Samuel 16:7). But we are absolutely commanded to judge the behavior of others when it comes to the principles that are to govern our lives as outlined in the Bible. This type of mutually agreed-upon accountability relationship is a treasure worth attaining to be sure and will no doubt take time, courage, and emotional energy to develop.

With the proper tools in hand, an understanding of how to use them, and the master Gardener by our side, we are prepared for the hard work this journey involves. We will find great success in forming new patterns of behavior that are pleasing to the Father, and those behaviors will affect every other relationship we have for the better. However, like any great journey, we will have moments on mountain peaks, walks on plateaus, and also treks through the meadow below. At various times, we will be tempted to drop both the tools and the Master's hand and travel the road alone, not only when the path is treacherous, but also when the travel is easier. We even may lose sight of the reasons we took the Father's hand in the first place. But after we have used the tools long enough, dropping them will seem unnatural, and stepping over them to leave the work behind will be too difficult to bear. The Holy Spirit will provide a niggling ache if we attempt it, and hopefully our church family will be a nuisance until we pick the tools up once again. To effectively tend the gardens of our hearts to redeem our childlikeness, we need to be developing a lifelong habit of regularly using the tools of Bible study, prayer, and fellowship with other believers until we end up with calluses on our hands and knees from the hard work.

# STUDY GUIDE

1. What aspects of your lifestyle or thought processes tend to be obstacles to your regularly reading the Bible and spending time in prayer?

2. Read Ecclesiastes 4:7–12. What do you read about the benefits of being in relationship with other believers?

3. Describe a time when you were fearful about joining a church or a small group.

4. How can interacting regularly with your heavenly Father be of benefit in interacting with others?

# CHAPTER 15

# RUN TO THE FATHER

After two successful years at the major-league level, we found ourselves with the Cincinnati Reds, who happened to have a surplus of pitchers at the beginning of spring training. It is interesting and not unrelated to note that I had earnestly prayed that Andy would have a fantastic spring and be selected as a member of the major-league team at the end of camp. I also had earnestly been praying throughout spring training for the Lord's help in solving a problem I knew I would face during the summer months. A dear childhood friend had asked me to be her matron of honor in her June wedding. I was thrilled to accept, but had to figure out how to fulfill that role with my nursing baby in tow. Among the options I had considered were taking my mother or a trusted babysitter along with me for the ceremony, to be held in Estes Park, Colorado. What I had not considered was that God may see fit to put me in close proximity to my friend during the months leading up to the wedding. But when the cuts were made, we were off to Denver, Colorado, where Andy would be playing triple-A baseball. Being back in the minor leagues was not exactly how I had envisioned my prayers being answered!

During those months in Denver, Andy and I were in a position of leadership among our teammates due to our age and experience at the major-league level. We had the opportunity to share our faith in the Lord through our words and our actions. Furthermore, I thoroughly enjoyed the extra time with my friend as I assisted in the preparations for her wedding day. When it came time for the wedding weekend, God used the wife of a team member to make our time even more special and comfortable. Her family owned a cabin in Estes Park, only a couple of miles from the hotel where I would be staying with the bride. Several of the wives made it a mommy-and-child weekend, and they collectively cared for my daughter while I was busy with wedding festivities. In spite of all my worrying, God's provision was perfect!

Shortly after the wedding, I received a call one afternoon from my husband, who was on a road trip. He excitedly told me he had been called back up to the major leagues and was on his way to Cincinnati. Needless to say, I was thrilled with the news, but the next hurdle was to figure out how to move our daughter, me, and our belongings across the country. As I hung up the phone, I was filled with a mixture of joy and sadness. I hated the part of baseball life that seemed to always leave me alone to pack, drive, and parent. I cried hard right there at the kitchen table and belatedly bowed my head to pray and ask the Lord to show me the way. While I was still praying, my phone rang, and God showed Himself to me in a very personal way.

On the phone was the wife of a Cincinnati team member who was one of my closest friends. She had heard the news of Andy's return to the big leagues and was calling to tell me how excited she was that I would be arriving in Cincinnati soon. Of course, I dumped my load of concern on her willing ears and expressed my dread of packing the car and driving with my child such a long distance. My friend patiently listened and then told me my needs had already been met.

She explained that the player my husband was replacing had been severely injured and planned to go home for the remainder of the season. He and his wife had asked if we would be willing to house-sit at their furnished condominium. Next, my friend told me a missionary from her church in Cincinnati had been in Denver for several weeks at a Christian conference and was praying for a way to get back to his home in Cincinnati without it costing too much. So at eight o'clock the next morning, a Christian brother arrived to pick up my fully packed car to drive it to Ohio. Then, at ten o'clock, my minister's wife picked my baby and me up to take us to the airport. Upon our arrival in Cincinnati, my friend met us and then took us to a beautiful, fully furnished temporary home. Complete with a high chair, a crib, and toys, the condo had been professionally cleaned and prepared for our arrival. I didn't even have to make beds or go to the grocery store!

I didn't necessarily always listen attentively, but even with my ineptitude, I learned my plans and God's are not always the same. I also learned His ways are always best! I was also reminded that the Lord desires to use His children in sharing the Good News of Jesus Christ with others and that His mission may have to override my desire to be someplace else. In addition, I witnessed God's ability to provide for my needs better than I ever could. In my childlike state, I was committed to the process of walking with my Father through life, and even with my limitations, I was able to receive His provisions. Our surrender to the Father hinges on our decision to do so, not on how good we are at doing so. That ability is always a work in progress. God looks at the heart, and I am personally very thankful that He can and does!

Jesus commanded that we "change and become like little children." He said this because He understood we would have experiences that we would allow to take us captive and effectively keep us bound in such a way that we would be unable to receive love in its purest form from the Father. From the beginning of time, God has desired a simple, relaxed, and unencumbered relationship with us, the prize of all of His creation. But sin got in the way. We read in Genesis about His evening stroll through the garden, calling to His children to come and walk with Him. Adam and Eve had sinned by disobeying God's specific instructions, and they felt the shame of that sin. So they hid from the Father. Since that time, mankind has struggled with the reality of sin and shame. Consequently, our childlikeness has become entangled with the weeds of sin, and our ability to freely relate to God has become hindered by the overgrowth of our shame. It doesn't seem to matter to the little child within each of us whether the shame we feel is a result of our own sin or the sin of another. The fact is that sin and shame have propelled us into a raging war between our flesh and our spirit, and therefore, our willingness to surrender to the authority of almighty God is left wanting. We struggle between doing life our own way and submitting to the capable ways of our God.

Now it is up to us to fight the battle between dependence and independence and, once we realize our need for Him, to run to the Father with enthusiasm. He is patiently waiting for us to permit Him access to our garden so the weeding, pruning, and new planting can begin.

As we seek to learn and grow while walking hand in hand with the master Gardener, and thereby develop a transparent relationship with Him, we will better understand that we should never question God's great love for His children! Of course, it is okay with Him if we do ask questions, as children are naturally inquisitive, and the Father certainly can handle our doubt. Naturally, the inquiry of a child is especially intense when he does not like the situation in which he finds himself or shudders at the unknowns in life. "Where are we going? Why? What's going to happen, and what am I going to get?" This is only the beginning when it comes to the questions a child can come up with at any given moment. For parents, naptime is useful for escaping this type of diatribe. Thankfully, God never tires of our questions when we ask them in earnest and when we are willing to listen to His reply. So one obstacle we may face in swinging the garden gate wide open in total surrender to the Father is our willingness to ask questions and hear His answers. Our natural temptation is to run away to figure out the answers and then let God know what needs to happen. However, on this journey with the Father toward childlikeness, the spirit part of our being must learn the art of listening to direction from Him instead.

In the first eleven years of my marriage, I had many opportunities to practice this particular lesson because we moved thirty-seven times—a minimum of three times a year to go to spring training, our teams' hometowns for the regular season, and then back to our home base again. Throw in a few trades and playing winter baseball in Puerto Rico, and the moves add up quickly. As a result, I was constantly asking God questions and was not so proficient at listening to Him. As a matter of survival, I learned to pack quickly and efficiently. I wish I could say I learned my lesson as fast when it came to waiting on His answers.

We learn along the way that the outcome of surrender is not always trauma and pain. Complete surrender also prepares the way for us to receive the fullest extent of the many blessings God has in store for those who choose to walk through life with Him. While oftentimes the anxiety I feel has no basis in reality, my distracted state might cause me to miss out on a sweet gift the Father desires to give to me. I must hold fast to the truth of His tender love and care for me and let go of those untrustworthy feelings that tend to lead me astray so quickly and easily.

I have a childhood memory of my unease in following my earthly father's instructions when my family was on a vacation in the Florida Keys and we had the opportunity to ride a dolphin in the ocean. One of my favorite childhood shows was *Flipper* because I thought it looked like so much fun to live on the coast and have a pet dolphin to play with all summer long. So I was extremely excited to participate in this activity . . . right up to the moment I was told to jump into the deep, dark ocean and wait for the dolphin to come get me. I will never forget the fear that consumed me as my mind ran rampant with images of all that could possibly come get me besides the dolphin. At that moment, it didn't cross my mind that many others had jumped into the water that day without incident. With much encouragement from my patient daddy, I finally took the plunge and experienced a wild ride while holding the fin of an obliging dolphin. I did receive a nasty scrape in the process—but it was because, in my panic over the frightening possibilities, I failed to follow the instructions to jump out far enough to avoid the barnacles on the dock. I suppose I was clinging to the false sense of security I felt staying close to shore. My dad cleaned and wrapped my wound, and I learned a valuable lesson that day about trusting my father's wisdom over my fickle feelings. Similarly, the Father knows things I don't know and sees things I don't see. He smiles when I am willing to place my trust in Him, and He cringes at my attempts to accept His blessing on my own terms.

We have the knowledge of God's love for His children, proof of His ability to provide, and assurance of His access to all resources. So why do we ever doubt? Why do we ever fret? We doubt, fret, worry, and question because we know that the circumstances we face will not always work out to our liking, and God will not always answer our prayers the way we like. So along with our struggle to ask our questions and listen for the answers, another obstacle we face in swinging that garden gate open to the Father is accepting the answer we hear.

We learn that the outcome of our complete surrender may pave the way for good times and abundant blessings in many forms, but it is also true that our fear and realization of potential pain sometimes may cause us to hold back. We may not have a clear and conscious thought about God's involvement in a situation, but we somehow have the notion that we may be able to do something more to fix a problem ourselves. After all, we think, life experience has proved that we don't always get what we desire when we leave the outcome in God's hands.

Personally, I prayed fervently for God to heal my daddy of a brain tumor with the absolute belief that He could do it, yet he died at age sixty-two.

My youngest child developed life-threatening allergies as a toddler that could result in respiratory arrest and death if he ingests the wrong food or medicine and doesn't get immediate help. And even though I have ardently prayed for God to remove this malady from his life, it remains and affects his lifestyle daily. My daughter suffered three miscarriages while I prayed without ceasing each time that a healthy baby would be born. When she became pregnant again, I pleaded with God for the outcome we all desired and got a knot in my stomach every time she called. I couldn't relax until I heard the lighthearted sweetness in her voice and knew everything was okay. Each time sadness, fear, and doubt assail me in any given moment, especially as it concerns those most dear to me, I have to deliberately and emphatically give my concerns back to my Father. I must remind myself constantly that He loves my husband, sons, daughters, grandchildren, parents, and anyone else I hold dear more than I can possibly imagine—and I have a very good imagination! Though these loved ones are my family, I do not have the capability to love them as my Father does because He is the Author of love, and they are His children!

But I have to be honest and say that these are the times when I'm not sure I want to surrender my will to His, if it means another miscarriage, a sick child, the death of someone I love, or some other devastating outcome. I certainly don't want to feel pain from watching someone I love suffer in any way. When I realize I cannot do any more than I am already doing, I sometimes go to the Father as a last resort, much like a child does when lost. The Father accepts me in my state of unrest and does not condemn me for my uncertainty. When I don't know what else to do, I deliberately let go of my agony by articulating my thoughts in prayer to the Father.

In the last five days of my mother's life, I stayed by her side constantly. I slept with her in her big bed the night she became very ill in order to be close to her and feel her presence. Much of that night, I simply watched her breathe and memorized the beauty of her face while already feeling the great loss in my life. Once she was in the hospital, I wanted to make sure she was comfortable and be there if she woke up. Most of all, it was important to me to be with her when she breathed her last breath. One time in those last few days, I left the hospital at the insistence of my family to take a shower and have a break from my vigil. While driving home, I was in my own world until a song came on the Christian radio station that articulated perfectly how I was feeling. While listening, I cried so hard that I had to pull over on the side of the road. I felt my heart was going to explode with the agony of my pain and the intense need to be in intimate closeness with my heavenly Father. The song was "Breathe," by Michael W. Smith, and the words, which express intense desperation for God, tore at and soothed my soul.

My family and friends' presence and expressions of affection were unbelievably soothing in the midst of such pain. But even the hugs from my husband and the tears I shed on his shoulder could not bring the relief I received from my deepest encounters with the Lord, which were so beautifully expressed in this song. When I experience these times of heartache and trepidation, I know my Father is willing, able, and waiting to provide the comfort I need as I place my trust in Him in a childlike way. He is always waiting! It's up to me to come.

As we do the hard work to surrender our will and our plans to God, we must learn how to surrender the essence of our very being to the Father. The only way I know to do this is to follow the lead of the psalmist who knowingly wrote about submitting to the Father's scrutiny in our lives. This is what he wrote at the end of Psalm 19: "Who can discern his errors? Forgive my hidden faults. Keep your servant also from willful sins; may they not rule over me. Then will I be blameless, innocent of great transgression. May the words of my mouth and the meditation of my heart be pleasing in your sight. O LORD, my Rock and my Redeemer" (vv. 12–14). Then, in Psalm 119:23–24, the psalmist comes before the Father in complete transparency and makes this request: "Search me, O God, and know my heart; test me and know my anxious thoughts. See if there is any offensive way in me, and lead me in the way everlasting." These verses shine a light on the real meaning of complete surrender. They state a recognition that we are not always capable of identifying our mistakes and that our willful, disobedient behavior can become a master in our lives. But the writer is pleading with the Father to search the dark, secluded places of his heart and illuminate them with His light so childlike purity can be attained once again.

We set off on this journey to follow the command Jesus gave His followers to "change and become like little children." We have investigated the possibility that life experience has altered us from our original childlike state and perhaps have even recognized a need to let God do some much-needed work in the gardens in our hearts. But the only way for us to achieve the type of well-tended garden that allows for unhindered interaction with our Father is to completely surrender everything to Him. And because submitting my will, my plans, and the core of my being to the care of the Father can be terrifying, or even seem impossible, we were not meant to enter into this venture alone. Remember, our responsibility is to invite Him to partner with us on the journey and to let the Father gently pry our hands off of what we hold so tightly.

Because communication is a key component in any relationship, the more we interact with Him along the way, the more we understand the truths He has been trying to share with us throughout the journey. We begin to see what He sees and want what He wants and love what He loves. At this point, it is easier for us to yield our plans for the journey because our level of trust has been deepened as our childlikeness has been recovered. But the task of releasing those plans is less problematic as we get a better grasp on the true identity of our Partner on the journey.

# STUDY GUIDE

1. Read James 1. What questions have you asked God lately?

2. Describe your behavior through the process of waiting for an answer.

3. What are you afraid to relinquish to the Father for fear the outcome may not be desirable to you?

4. What are you learning about God right now that will help you with the letting-go process?

# CHAPTER 16
# RUN WITH THE LEADER

As the wife of a professional baseball player, I remember feeling so helpless and frustrated one season when my husband was not put in a game for weeks for no apparent reason. A relief pitcher, Andy was typically used on a fairly regular basis. He was pitching exceptionally well that year and gaining much success on the mound when his manager seemingly forgot him at game time. After about a week, Andy went to his manager's office to find out why but, unfortunately, left with no answers.

During that time, what I remember most is that my husband, while aggravated and confused, continued to practice and work out daily without interruption. He had a great deal of respect for his manager and chose to trust his authority even without understanding his decisions on the field. Andy did his workout in the afternoons as if nothing was different. Late in each game, when he was sure he wouldn't be used that night, he would throw on the sidelines to keep his skills sharp. More than two and a half weeks had elapsed when he was finally called into a game. His performance was exceptional; he struck out five of the six batters he faced in two innings pitched!

When circumstances are not to our liking, like Andy did in baseball, we would be wise to look at the situation as an opportunity to "practice" our surrender to our very capable Father. We must "work out" every day by choosing to accept His wisdom over our vague understanding. We must work diligently to keep our "skills" sharp. Indeed, it is so hard sometimes! Human nature is such that we like to have immediate answers, and we do not like to suffer emotionally, physically, or financially. Actually, to state it plainly, we prefer for life to go along comfortably and without any surprises or interruptions to our well-made plans.

Therefore, we will not always like the twists, turns, and hills on the trail of life. But we can remain confident in God as our leader, as we are not traveling with a haphazard guide; rather, the King of the universe is in the lead. But it does not make sense for us to submit to someone we do not recognize as an authority figure. For example, a law-abiding citizen will pull over when blue lights are flashing, and an employee understands he must do what his boss says if he wants to keep his job. Also, a professional athlete must submit to the wishes of his manager, coaches, and front office if he is to remain employed. While the driver, employee, or baseball player may go through the proper chains of command if being treated unfairly, there still exists an understanding of proper respect for the authority figure.

Likewise, it is our responsibility to recognize God's ultimate authority over all of creation, which, of course, includes you and me! In the Bible, we are instructed to let creation be a testimony to His eternal power and divine nature. To remember what we have been taught or discover this truth for the first time, we must use the tools discussed previously. This quest should involve intense Bible study, passionate seeking through prayer, and a determined effort to receive guidance from other committed and trusted Christians. Don't forget the imperative to listen closely to the Holy Spirit for discernment, guidance, and confirmation of His presence in our lives. After all, the Lord God Almighty will always reveal Himself to anyone who earnestly and humbly seeks to know Him.

The path we are on with the Father is a personal one; therefore, the plans He has for each one of His children are personal as well. When we remember that the journey is all about a personal relationship, we can understand a bit better how the Father can have a personal plan for the gardens of our hearts and how the fruit produced there can be beautiful and sweet. Like our lives, gardens are charted out by a gardener who takes into account every component that will influence the outcome. Four different seasons are considered each year. Fertilizer will need to be applied, and pruning must take place, but at the appropriate times. If a certain type of insect or fungus becomes a problem, a remedy is applied. Older plants will be uprooted, and new ones will be planted. Some plants will need to be placed in the shade, while others need more sunlight. The arrangement of the entire garden is in order as the gardener applies his knowledge of each plant to the overall plan. This involves much more than a casual observer's limited view notices.

Likewise, our heavenly Father is our master Gardener, who has a plan for each of His children that is designed based on who He created us to be and who we have become as a result of our choices and experiences. He understands that the free will He has given to mankind inevitably will mean we will be hurt, betrayed, and mistreated by the folly of others. He is also aware that we will sometimes decide to do life our own way, without regard for His instructions or the relationship He wants with us. At any given moment, the Father is ready to receive the injured child and begin on a fresh, newly charted course that will bring inner peace and beauty back to that child and will give purpose to his life. All we need to do is run back to the Father in humility as we acknowledge the authority of the God we serve.

A wonderful example is the apostle Paul, whose life account is found in the New Testament. Before his face-to-face encounter with Jesus, Paul had been a rule-following Jew and a radical persecutor of the church that had begun as a result of the life and teachings of Jesus. Of course, this means Paul's beliefs were diametrically opposed to any of Jesus' teachings. But after a personal meeting with Jesus, Paul made a U-turn in his life journey and became a sold-out follower of Jesus and His teachings. In this face-to-face encounter, Paul became acutely aware that Jesus is the Christ, and he was standing in the presence of almighty God Himself. Paul's submission to His authority was immediate and complete!

For the rest of Paul's life, he suffered numerous horrific consequences of his vivacious and tenacious efforts in sharing the truths of his newfound faith in Jesus Christ with everyone who would listen. But he stayed the course even when he faced extreme adversity. Paul tells it like this: "Five times I received from the Jews the forty lashes minus one. Three times I was beaten with rods, once I was stoned, three times I was shipwrecked, I spent a night and a day in the open sea, I have been constantly on the move. I have been in danger from rivers, in danger from bandits, in danger from my own countrymen, in danger from Gentiles; in danger in the city, in danger in the country, in danger at sea; and in danger from false brothers. I have labored and toiled and have often gone without sleep; I have known hunger and thirst and have often gone without food; I have been cold and naked. Besides everything else, I face daily the pressure of my concern for all the churches" (2 Corinthians 11:24–28).

Paul understood that the Father had authority over him and had given him a specific task to accomplish that would use every ounce of the same God-given abilities that he previously used for his own purposes. Because of Paul's complete surrender to his Master, he was given the privilege of tapping into the power in the life, death, burial, and resurrection of the Christ! This did not keep him from suffering, but it did provide him with grace and strength from the Lord that enabled him to handle everything in a way that pleased almighty God and brought purpose to his existence.

In his obedience to God, the apostle Paul not only dealt with great external adversity, but he also tells of personal adversity he called a "thorn in his flesh," which he prayed to the Father to remove. The account given in the Bible does not tell of the specific ailment he suffered, but no doubt Paul wanted it gone. However, God chose to leave this "thorn," and there is no indication that Paul understood why. When faced with the disappointment of this unanswered prayer, we see a mature man of the faith choosing to keep his trust securely in the Father instead of expressing anger and rebellion. Though he did not receive what he requested, Paul continued to trust and surrender to the One in authority over him. In his account of this experience, Paul acknowledged that the ailment helped him better understand how his weakness allowed for God's strength to fill him. Paul realized that God's strength was supremely preferable to his own.

Paul experienced humility, desperation, and dependence on our Lord for everything, which resulted in an unwavering devotion to the God he willingly served. Paul really seemed to understand that the only means of coping with life's ups and downs was through an intimate relationship with the Person of Jesus Christ. Note that he was focused on strengthening this relationship, rather than on obeying a well-known set of rules that outlined his faith.

Like Paul, we can all learn to be content on the trail even when it gets bumpy and we face tragedy, suffering, and extreme pain. We can do this by recognizing the authority of the One with whom we travel and by trusting the plan He has for our journey. Perhaps it would be more convenient, and infinitely more preferable, to swing by the general store along the way and purchase this contentment than to struggle through the learning process. But if we are willing to do this, we will soon find, like the apostle Paul, that wrestling with the uncertainty and discomfort will serve to strengthen the connection we have with the Father. The alternative to surrender is a haughty rejection of our Leader and His plan, which will only bring alienation from the Father and opens wide the gates of the gardens in our hearts for the enemy, whose intent is to bring about our destruction. But because the disconnect we experience is of our own making, we can undo it by making a simple U-turn back to the One who is always waiting for the return of His wayward child.

# STUDY GUIDE

1. Read Psalm 19. Describe God as the almighty Creator. Now describe Him as the personal God who cares for us as individuals.

2. Make a list of the benefits of meditating on God's Word, the Bible.

3. What in your past or present is keeping you from trusting the Father as your Leader?

# CHAPTER 17

# RUNNING REQUIRES REST

In the craziness of this world, we may easily become distracted and find it difficult to stay on track. However, we must get in the habit of recognizing that we are always in the presence of God and learning how to be inwardly still in His presence. Every hour of every day, we must acquire the skill of letting our relationship with the Father be the next thought on our minds. In this way, no matter what occurs outwardly in the course of our day, we will turn to the Father and say a prayer of thanksgiving or lift up a plea for help and remain confident that He hears our prayer in that moment.

No doubt, it is difficult to learn the art of being still. We require young children to take a nap because we know they need it. When they wake up, they are refreshed and energized. So why do we not recognize our need for quiet and rest? Rest comes in many forms, but I am talking about the kind of rest that is simple stillness in the wake of our complete surrender to the Father. We may be familiar with the command "Be still, and know that I am God" (Psalm 46:10). My favorite part of the psalm begins in verse 2, which says, "Therefore we will not fear, though the earth give way and the mountains fall into the heart of the sea." Verse 6 states, "Nations are in uproar." I love that God understands my aversion to and need for stillness in the midst of the chaos of my life. In fact, in times of turmoil, my natural tendency is to make a plan fast and get to work. So this type of stillness has to be what I choose, though, like every other aspect of childlikeness, it is hard work to hold fast to that choice.

Creation, including gardens and woods, used as analogies throughout this book, is not only a great reminder of God's existence, authority, power, and presence; it is a wonderful means of experiencing stillness within ourselves. In Romans, chapter 1, we are told that creation reflects the eternal power and divine nature of God. If we think about it, there is no place we can go to separate ourselves from something He has created . . . because He created us. Yes, even our bodies are a wonder to observe. The wonder of God's creation has the ability to render us speechless, which, by the way, is not a bad thing. Being silent and still before God is a useful method for hearing His voice in our spirit with clarity.

When I am in the mountains, in just one hour while sitting on the porch, I can observe countless aspects of nature that scream of the awesomeness of our God! I hear numerous birds with different calls and see a woodpecker, hummingbird, robin, and hawk. I observe bumblebees, wasps, flies, and butterflies, among other things, in the sky. I see the less attractive insects, such as ants and spiders. I see squirrels, turkeys, and chipmunks. I hear the wind blowing through the trees and the creek splashing across the rocks beyond the meadow. Then, just before my hour is ended, I see a little fawn nestled next to a tree and its mother, along with several other yearlings, in the thicket beyond. How often do we see or hear these wonders and go about our daily lives without thinking of God? We ought to notice creation around us and think of Him every day. We may not see all those creatures, but we do see the sun, the sky, birds, and foliage, and can reflect on the One who put them there.

Observe the wonder a child expresses when looking at something new to him in nature. We love taking our grandson to the beach because the shells and sea life are so exciting to him. We took some adult friends from Canada to the beach when they visited Florida for the first time, and their faces reflected that same wonder we see on Tristan's face. I remember how I felt the first time I saw the Grand Canyon and the Rocky Mountains. Snorkeling in the Cayman Islands was an exhilarating experience, as I saw underwater life that I had not had the joy of seeing before. I enjoyed the years we had a saltwater aquarium in our home because watching a rare beauty would always create a sense of calm in me.

The concepts of utter stillness and complete surrender coexist quite nicely if we stop to contemplate their meaning. When one company of soldiers surrenders to another, I am sure slow and deliberate movement is involved. When a crime suspect surrenders to police, he comes out with his hands raised and taking cautious steps. When our Jack Russell terrier surrenders to my husband's authority, he rolls over on his back and then doesn't move.

As we learn to let surrender and calmness mingle in our lives, what we come to understand is that we will find the quickest path to freedom in relinquishing control and cherishing the tranquility that follows. Great release can be found in letting the Father be in charge. My bent is toward leadership, and I find it hard to stay in the background if a clear-cut leader has not been designated. I especially struggle when chaos exists because I like things to be orderly. But I never have to worry about the quality of leadership found in almighty God! He knows what He's doing, and chaos will only be present if He wants it to be, so I can relax and follow the Master in worshipful submission.

Our son Joshua expressed a beautiful understanding of the concept of surrender, calmness, and silence in his answer to "Is silence really golden?" He wrote the following thoughts in response to this question:

> *This silly question came to my mind immediately after I had stopped playing some worship music while alone in my room. With a final strum on my guitar, I closed my eyes and let the note just ring out until it was too small to hear. My mind drifted many different ways as I sat alone. I focused on the sounds, words, emotions, and thoughts that were coursing through my veins. In this great silence, I had a chance*

to meditate on what God really wanted from me and where He was leading me. While sitting in dead silence, I was hesitant to make a sound because I didn't want to spoil that incredible opportunity God had given to me.

It was at that exact moment that it hit me. It nearly took my breath away. I began to realize that for the first time in a long time, I was truly, honestly, and humbly in the presence of God in the act of worship! For those who have experienced this, it is not always comfortable to be in this realm of vulnerability, and it is tempting to look for an out. But even though I felt exposed, I kept silent in the midst of God. With my eyes closed, mouth shut, and heart open, I opened myself up to the incredible love of God. This was awesome! I felt God's presence surround me. The only thing I could think to do was just stay quiet and listen for anything He might say. While I didn't hear an audible voice, I do believe beyond the shadow of a doubt that what God wants from us, as Christians, is to have the faith to sit in a silent room, away from distractions, and just listen for His voice. This whole experience was incredibly uplifting. Above all else, one thing has run through my mind while writing this: **Silence is not golden; silence is godly!**

# STUDY GUIDE

1. Read Psalm 46. What chaotic events are described in this psalm?

2. What has kept you from being still and silent before God in your personal moments of chaos?

3. What benefits have you experienced from choosing stillness or can imagine experiencing if you do so?

4. Look around at this moment. What do you see that has been created by God? Spend a few moments practicing just being in His presence, right where you are. Perhaps begin with words of thanksgiving for what He has created.

# CHAPTER 18

# RUNNING TO THE END

If the object of our affection is the Father, we have hopefully learned some good tips for practicing the basics of developing an intimate relationship with Him. Hunger for a deeper connection is consuming us, ridiculous excitement about what is ahead to discover is making us giddy, and we are eager to be on our way. It is vital that we remember we don't have to get our problems all figured out and cleaned up first. In doing so, we would miss the point. And we cannot possibly understand the Father's amazing love from across an expanse like the vastness of a large field. Instead, this is a very real and personal relationship that can only be experienced when one hand is grasped in another for the adventure. Run with abandon first, and then the journey really begins!

Once we decide to go on this lifelong journey, we must have focus and determination to get a running start. But once we reach a good pace and we've developed a rhythm to our trek, it becomes easier to maintain. However, we will need to renew our commitment to the journey often. It will be awkward and uncomfortable as we struggle through the early stages of our education. But with persistence, we will begin to grasp a better understanding of the goal and the obstacles we will need to overcome to reach the goal. With that new understanding, we will become more confident in our steps.

When we remain committed to the journey we have begun, we find we become a little more like our Companion each day. While the phrase "you are what you eat" disturbs me because the mental picture is not attractive, the picture can be one of beauty when we consume the things of God. Read through the Bible, and write down traits of the almighty One, with whom we may choose to walk. Bread of Life, Refuge, Savior, Fortress, Redeemer, Rock, Deliverer, Provider, Healer, Creator, Righteousness, Most High, and Lover of my Soul are just a few of the descriptions of our Companion on this journey toward childlikeness. To discipline our minds, we must nourish ourselves by ravenously devouring this type of food for the soul! Then, we will love becoming what we eat! Then we, and those around us, will notice a distinct difference in our inner and outer appearance. As we walk with the Father and let Him be our sustenance, we find that our thoughts and motives are purer, our speech is more pleasing to those who listen, and our actions reflect the heart of the One with whom we journey.

Our oldest son, Drew, had an assignment that was an "experiential exercise." I have received his permission to print his words, which reflect an appreciation for his earthly father's companionship on life's journey:

### A Leader in My Life

*I am becoming my father, and I could not be happier. My father is the single greatest leader in my life, bar none. I love my dad. He has been actively involved in helping me to become a stronger, wiser, and better man since day one.*

*I could not begin to enumerate the lessons, skills, goals, and characteristics that my father's leadership in my life has established in me. They are legion. Rather, I will present a single, demonstrable example:*

*Since the time I learned to talk, my father has been teaching me to speak. Logic, critical thinking, problem solving, and debate have been part of everyday life with my father for as long as I can remember. He wanted me to have not only autonomy and intellectual strength, but also moral integrity and wisdom. He wanted me to know what I believed and why I believed it. Furthermore, I had to be able to articulate my position. Debates on various topics were and still are a family pastime. Just for fun, we will argue point and counterpoint until a clear winner is established. Even after a real dispute over a real issue, my parents often would still take the time to discuss my language with me and critique my rhetoric and arguments. "Don't use so many absolutes in your argument; they're often difficult to prove conclusively." "Try not to let your emotions dictate your speech." "A wise man always thinks what he says. A fool always says what he thinks." "Work on communicating, not just talking. Using appropriate words, articulate your thoughts into the best, most understandable message." "Eye contact!" . . . In this way, my father has led me to become a proficient communicator.*

*I am thankful for my father's leadership in my life because today I am very, very happy, and I know why. I have done what he has led me to do, and I am who he has shaped me to become. I'm not perfect, but I'm always working toward a goal my father taught me to pursue.*

*God has given me this day to do as I will. I can waste it or use it for good. What I do today is very important because what I trade for it is a day of my life. When tomorrow comes this day will be gone forever, leaving behind something I've traded for it. I want it to be gain, not loss . . . good, not evil . . . success, not failure . . . in order that I should never regret the price I paid for it. This day is my day to move ahead.*

*Now my days are full of life, my nights are full of peace, and my future is bright with promise. Thank you, Dad.*

"I have done what he has led me to do, and I am who he has shaped me to become. I'm not perfect, but I'm always working toward a goal my father taught me to pursue." Although written about his dad, Drew's words depict the essence of an appropriate longing to see the effects of the hand of our heavenly Father in our lives. We can realize the desired result when we renew our complete surrender to Him often, even daily.

One outcome of this renewed daily journey is we will become increasingly free of the many things that have kept us enslaved with each step we take. Also, we will begin to implement what we have learned along the way so we keep our childlikeness in a healthy state. This is not to say we will never have a stray weed or an unclipped branch invade our garden because those will continue to plague us as long as we draw breath. But it does mean we can now hear the voice of the Father with clarity! He has so much to tell us now that we are still and ready to listen. Now He will be able to continually reveal to us His specific and personally designed plan and give us the ability to see it through. We will have the fresh opportunity to choose to work hand in hand with the Father for His eternal purposes. Our personal world is a mission field, and we are the perfectly prepared missionaries for that particular field! I cannot think of a better way to experience freedom than to know we are living in obedience to the will of our heavenly Father.

Another outcome of our daily walk with the Father is we will worry less about what other people think because we care more about the opinion of our travel Partner. The sometimes incorrect conclusions others draw about our lives become less important as we stay in constant communication with the One whose opinion matters. We may listen to the input of others concerning our walk with the Lord and how it plays out in other relationships, but now we are better able to discern whether the input lines up with the Father's truth. The Holy Spirit's living within us is like a water-filtering system that removes impurities from what we ingest. When others make judgment calls about our lives or our character, the correct course of action is to put it through that filtering system to ascertain the level of truth. Keep in mind that no one knows our thoughts and motives better than the One with whom we journey each day. And if pride or any other weed creeps into our hearts, it can be uprooted quickly as we continue daily to humbly submit to the pruning at the hand of the master Gardener.

As we daily reclaim our childlikeness and radically submit to the ongoing shaping at the hand of our loving Father, we are truly able to say without reservation that God is good. Furthermore, our confidence in that statement will not waver when we don't like the way life is playing out. Even when the hard times seem unbearable, our tendency now will be to depend entirely upon the Father for even our next breath.

My mother faced a five-year battle with cancer, and when the end came, it came swiftly. In just a matter of days, she progressed from feeling relatively fine to sleeping and talking little, and then slipping into a peaceful sleep for two days before her death. The last day my mom was awake provides a beautiful illustration of complete surrender and reliance upon the Lord in a simple, childlike manner for one's every need.

When mom awoke that Saturday morning, it was her first full day in the hospital, and I was with her in the room. I leaned over and kissed her forehead, and she uttered, "I love you." I walked to the window to open the blinds, letting the morning sun brighten the room. Speaking seemed to be difficult for Mom, but I heard her weakly saying the words "This ... this ... this is the day ...." I was filled with momentary panic at the thought that my mother may be trying to tell me this was the moment she would leave me. However, she finished her thought with a faint, but confident, smile on her face. She recited one of her favorite verses, in Psalm 118: "This is the day the LORD has made; let us rejoice and be glad in it" (v. 24). The peace that filled my heart and mind at that moment was overwhelming. Upon observing my mom's countenance, I could see she was experiencing the same incredible peace.

Sleep came and went during the day, but as family and friends came to visit, my mom would open her eyes and do her best to express her love for each one of them. Late in the morning, one of her dearest friends entered the room after driving all night to see her. When she opened her eyes in greeting, she tried to speak once again. At first, the words did not come easily or quickly, but she said, "Trust . . . trust . . . trust . . . ." As we waited in anticipation for Mom to complete her thought to her friend, the words from Proverbs 3:5–6 suddenly flowed from her lips: "Trust in the LORD with all your heart and lean not on your own understanding; in all your ways acknowledge him, and he will make your paths straight." As everyone in the room cried and hugged in our tender grief, Mom fell back into a peaceful sleep.

During the afternoon, Mom awakened occasionally and answered questions with a simple yes or no. And she was able to say "I love you" to those who hugged her in greeting. In the early evening, when her doctor came in for a visit, we all had the distinct impression that he came to say good-bye to a special patient.

When he entered the room, he sat by her bedside and took her hand in his. Mom was not responsive and seemed to be sleeping soundly. He spoke words of appreciation and admiration for her handling the cancer battle with a positive attitude. He knew of her strong faith in the Lord and, in fact, was a believer himself. He thanked my mom for living in such a way that had served as an example that helped strengthen his personal faith. As he stood to leave, we were all unsure whether she heard his precious words. But then, my mom squeezed the doctor's hand and opened her eyes. She looked into his eyes and said, "God is good." She closed her eyes once again, and the doctor sat back down by her bedside. These were my mom's final words in this life.

I believe the utterance of those verses throughout that day were one of the ways the Lord brought comfort to my mom as she existed between this world and her heavenly home. I am equally certain that they brought comfort to the rest of us who were privileged to hear them. The biblical words of assurance delivered from my mom's lips that day were like a warm blanket wrapped around an unsettled child by loving arms, offering a safe place to rest.

I believe when my mom left her fleshly body in that hospital room, she was prepared to run with abandon into the arms of her loving heavenly Father. She probably ran with such force that she knocked Him over, but neither one of them likely cared because she was listening to His voice as He said, "Welcome home, my precious child! I love you with all that I AM."

It is a requirement for all of us as followers of Jesus to aim to love the Lord with all of our heart, soul, mind, and strength and to love others as we love ourselves. But the degree of success we have in accomplishing that goal will depend upon our willingness to let go of our ties to this life. While Jesus was teaching one day, a rich young man approached Him and asked what good things he must do to receive eternal life. When Jesus told him to obey the commands of God, the young man's response was he had faithfully kept them since his childhood. Then, to his great surprise and disappointment, Jesus told him to go and sell everything he owned, give it to the poor, and come back to journey with Him. The Bible tells us the man went away sad because he had great wealth. We must clearly understand that the wealth in itself was not the problem, but the young man's attachment to that wealth was. Our ties to this life may, in fact, be our material possessions. But the tie that keeps us in bondage to this earthly life could just as easily be another person, our work, the power we wield, or even our ministry. For some the culprit may be a healthy body, financial security, or perhaps the desire for a God-honoring marriage. In and of themselves, these can be healthy life goals. But a stumbling block is before us if we misplace our passion to attain these goals above all else—including a relationship with the Father. We would be making the same mistake the rich young man made the day he spoke to Jesus. The list is endless when it comes to the things we can allow to become more important to us than a simple, relaxed, and unencumbered relationship with our heavenly Father!

If we are wise, we will look at the struggle the young man faced in attaining his desired goal of eternal life and ask ourselves a pointed question: Is God everything to me, or do I need just one thing more to be content? If the answer is the belief that God is everything to us, the next probing questions are: Am I willing to let go of everything, if that is what the Lord requires of me? Can I give God permission to do whatever it takes in my life to make me pliable to His shaping or to accomplish kingdom purposes that I don't understand? If I want to be wholly His, I will need to release the hold I have on all of my treasures and trust them to God's safekeeping. These treasures include my possessions, goals, comforts, dreams, and loved ones.

Let's ponder the possibilities of this point for a moment. Do I really trust God enough to gather up my gold, silver, and anything of value and put it in my car to drive to the appropriate vendor? It will require humility and resolve as the items are offered for sale and stamina to follow through once a price is agreed upon. Do I really trust God enough to let go of the people I hold dear to the care of the Father because He would rather I love them as an outpouring of Him than through my own efforts? Am I willing to trust Him in the face of longstanding bad health, or even a terminal illness, because I believe in the Father's ability to use my situation to bring others into eternal life as I confidently claim it for myself? Am I willing to graciously accept unemployment, singleness, poverty, pain, or even persecution for my faith because my hope is in the Lord, rather than these events of life?

We may feel safe answering yes, as it may seem way out in left field, so to speak, in the realm of possibilities. But I personally know people who have said yes to these questions and then had to face these circumstances. Some did not stay on the course of facing these tragedies or losses while holding the hand of the Father, and the result was utter devastation. I have seen others face similar conditions while endeavoring to cling to the Father, and the outcome was complete peace, unimaginable joy, and a sense of overwhelming love as they walked the path of suffering. They have experienced the comfort and security that comes from living in childlikeness with the Father. I have seen faithful Christians live through the heartache of the death of a child. I have been witness to others who survived the dread of lost relationships because their partners walked away from a moral life. I have walked through the valley with those who lost all financial resources, through no fault of their own, and were called by God to transition from a life of abundance to a life of scraping together pennies to pay the bills. Those who have faithfully journeyed through life's most difficult circumstances have recognized and clung to the truth that everything in this life is temporal, and real value is found only in following Jesus at any cost!

Is God my *everything*? It is imperative that we ask ourselves this question and open our minds wide to search out the honest answer. Wherever we find ourselves on the vast field of possibilities, our next step is to submit to the process of reclaiming our childlike traits so we can accept the pruning and reshaping we need at the hand of our loving heavenly Father. If we choose to obey the command Jesus gave to us to "change and become like little children" and are willing to pursue and cut loose whatever hinders our change, we will find that we are already liberated from that entanglement and are free to run with abandon to the Father to enjoy the journey of a lifetime. One day, we will enter the heavenly realm, be embraced by the Father, and finally understand the depth of love and utter delight He has for each of His children!

# STUDY GUIDE

1. What is your response to the challenge to "change and become like little children"?

2. Review the list of childlike traits that you made at the end of chapter 5. Are you aware of the childlike traits that have diminished in your life and have affected your relationship with the Father? If so, write some ideas as to how you will reclaim the top three traits on the list.

3. What freedoms would you like to experience as you continue on this journey with the Father?

4. Read Mark 10:17–31. What hinders your complete surrender to the Father? What do you need to "sell" in order to follow Jesus?

# IF YOU'RE A FAN OF THIS BOOK, PLEASE TELL OTHERS...

- Write about *Run with Abandon* on your blog, Twitter, MySpace, and Facebook page.

- Suggest *Run with Abandon* to friends.

- When you're in a bookstore, ask them if they carry the book. The book is available through all major distributors, so any bookstore that does not have *Run with Abandon* in stock can easily order it.

- Write a positive review of *Run with Abandon* on www.amazon.com.

- Send my publisher, HigherLife Publishing, suggestions on Web sites, conferences, and events you know of where this book could be offered at media@ahigherlife.com.

- Purchase additional copies to give away as gifts.

## CONNECT WITH ME...

To learn more about *Run with Abandon*, please contact me at:

> Jill McGaffigan
>
> www.runwithabandon.com
>
> runwithabandon.jill@gmail.com

You may also contact my publisher directly:

> HigherLife Publishing
>
> 400 Fontana Circle
>
> Building 1 – Suite 105
>
> Oviedo, Florida 32765
>
> Phone: (407) 563-4806
>
> Email: media@ahigherlife.com